X6

£3-95 NN

D0494641

Touchstones 4

A TEACHING ANTHOLOGY

Revised and expanded edition

MICHAEL AND PETER BENTON

HODDER AND STOUGHTON
LONDON SYDNEY AUCKLAND TORONTO

First published in Great Britain 1968
Second edition 1970
Third edition 1988
Second impression 1989

© 1968, 1988 M. G. Benton and P. Benton

ISBN 0 340 40823 9

All rights reserved. No part of this publication may be reproduced or transmitted in
any form or by any means, electronic or mechanical, including photocopy,
recording, or any information storage and retrieval system, without permission in
writing from the publisher or under licence from the Copyright Licensing Agency
Limited. Further details of such licences (for reprographic reproduction) may be
obtained from the Copyright Licensing Agency Limited, of 33–34 Alfred Place,
London WC1E 7DP.

Printed in Great Britain for
Hodder and Stoughton Educational
a division of Hodder and Stoughton Ltd
Mill Road, Dunton Green, Sevenoaks, Kent
by St Edmundsbury Press Ltd
Bury St Edmunds, Suffolk
Photoset by Rowland Phototypesetting Ltd
Bury St Edmunds, Suffolk

Contents

4

To the Teacher

Since the first *Touchstones* series was launched there have been major changes in teaching methods and many exciting new poets writing for children have emerged. We have revised the series so that the basic concept of the 'teaching anthology' remains. This is still the most effective way of combining three key features: an up-to-date selection of poems; teaching approaches which are primarily concerned with the individual's responses; and activities —often in pairs or small groups—which will bring the poems off the page. While many of the poems in the original volumes are retained, we have been able to include a generous selection of verse from current writers. The teaching sections on 'Exploring Poems' and the activities suggested at the end of each group of poems in the 'Anthology' have been completely revised and expanded. Even so, books can only do so much; poetry lessons, in particular, depend for their success upon a sympathetic relationship between teacher and pupils. When this exists children can learn more about what language is and what language does from experiencing poetry than from any other form of language use. What is more, approached creatively—with ample opportunities for performance and individual involvement—poetry lessons can be fun for both teacher and pupils.

The pattern of our 'teaching anthology' is as follows. First, in 'Exploring Poems' (Part A), we introduce three main topics which give information about a particular aspect of poetry, illustrate by examples and engage the children in talking, reading, and writing about poems. The individual teacher is the best judge of just how and when to use this area of the book. Secondly, in the 'Anthology' (Part B), we have grouped the material so that the teacher will be able to deal with several poems, linked by some common quality of technique, subject matter, style or attitude, in any one lesson or sequence of lessons. Thirdly, at the end of each section in the 'Anthology' we have provided suggestions for encouraging the pupils to respond to the poems in a variety of ways: live performances, tape-recordings, personal writing, displays and so on. We consider that pupils should be offered the chance to experiment, to play with the words, sounds and shapes of poems in the same way that they play with paints and materials in an art lesson. Unless it is developed, such freedom can become mere licence. Teachers, therefore, will often want to help children redraft their first ideas. Ideally, the 'play' element leads to a delight in the discipline of form.

Opportunities for this kind of personal involvement offer children both a means of understanding and ways of developing a 'feel' for poems which are not only enjoyable in themselves but also provide the best foundation for a fuller appreciation of poetry in later years.

Finally, we hope it is evident from the approaches we adopt that we do not wish the books to be followed slavishly as a 'course'. Indeed, the distinction between material suited, for example, to a fourth as opposed to a third form must sometimes be arbitrary. Although the books are numbered from one to five and the topics and poems have been chosen to suit particular age groups, teachers will find sufficient flexibility in the arrangement to be able to select and modify the material according to their own tastes and the abilities of their pupils. We also suggest the building up of resources to complement our selections. A mini-library of slim volumes of poetry chosen by author is essential in any school; and there are hundreds of practical ideas in the following books:

Michael Benton and Geoff Fox: *Teaching Literature 9–14*, OUP

Michael and Peter Benton : *Examining Poetry*, Hodder & Stoughton

Peter Benton : *Pupil, Teacher, Poem*, Hodder & Stoughton

Sandy Brownjohn : *Does it Have to Rhyme?* Hodder & Stoughton
What Rhymes with Secret? Hodder & Stoughton

Ted Hughes : *Poetry in the Making*, Faber

Michael Rosen : *I See a Voice*, Hutchinson

Stephen Tunnicliffe : *Poetry Experience*, Methuen

PART A

Exploring Poems

Images

(i) Reading with eye and ear

If you can imagine something you make a mental picture of it—a mental image. Both writing and reading depend upon these mental images. When *reading* a poem or a story you will often have been aware of pictures in your mind's eye, maybe of a place or a person, or of some incident that the words are describing. Think for a moment, too, about any stories or poems you have *written* and you will probably bring them to mind through 'picturing' in your head. You may well know already the word-pictures of haiku poems (see p. 52). 'Picture' suggests something that does not move but many images in poems are more than just 'stills'—they may create sounds or suggest tastes or smells or, as in the following example, describe things moving.

From Movements

Lark drives invisible pitons* in the air
And hauls itself up the face of space.
Mouse stops being comma and clockworks on the floor.
Cats spill from walls. Swans undulate through clouds.
Eel drills through darkness its malignant face.

Fox, smouldering through the heather bushes, bursts
A bomb of grouse. A speck of air grows thick
And is a hornet. When a gannet dives
It's a white anchor falling. And when it lands
Umbrella heron becomes walking-stick.

NORMAN MacCAIG

*peg or spike driven into rock to support climber or rope

11

Images are a kind of shorthand. If they work for us they give us a clear picture.

—Which of these images of creatures moving did you see most clearly in your mind's eye?

—Were there any that you did not see?

How is the feeling of spring created in the following lines? Read them through quietly to yourself and then *in pairs*, take it in turns to speak the lines aloud. At first, they may seem like a tongue-twister! Take care, the rhythms, sounds and stresses are tricky.

From Spring

Nothing is so beautiful as spring—
    When weeds, in wheels, shoot long and lovely and lush;
    Thrush's eggs look little low heavens, and thrush
Through the echoing timber does so rinse and wring
The ear, it strikes like lightnings to hear him sing;
    The glassy peartree leaves and blooms, they brush
    The descending blue; that blue is all in a rush
With richness; the racing lambs too have fair their fling.

GERARD MANLEY HOPKINS

Talk with your partner about what you *saw* and *heard* when you read these lines.

We all use images in our everyday speech—usually without being aware that this is what they are. We try to create vivid pictures in the minds of our listeners: 'He slammed the ball home!'; 'They dawdled along at a snail's pace.' In fact, animal images are used very commonly to describe the way human beings behave.

    In the poem over the page the writer describes men admiring a girl in an open-air tea-garden in Egypt. He has some fun at their expense by picturing them as different kinds of fish. Three groups could rehearse a performance. You will need:
– someone to mime the girl (eating ice-cream, tending her nails and so on);
– a narrator to read verses 1 and 2 of the last verse;
– 'an important fish' (vs. 3);
– a crustacean (vs. 4);
– a mackerel (vs. 5);
– a flatfish (vs. 5);
– and two or three others to suggest a shoal (vs. 6) – perhaps nine in all.

Divide up the lines and think about how you will present your reading.

Behaviour of Fish in an Egyptian Tea-Garden

As a white stone draws down the fish
she on the seafloor of the afternoon
draws down men's glances and their cruel wish
for love. Her red lip on the spoon

slips in a morsel of ice-cream. Her hands
white as a shell, are submarine
fronds sinking with spread fingers, lean
along the table, carmined at the ends.

A cotton magnate, an important fish
with great eyepouches and golden mouth
through the frail reefs of furniture swims out
and idling, suspended, stays to watch.

A crustacean old man, clamped to his chair
sits near her and might coldly see
her charms through fissures where the eyes should be;
or else his teeth are parted in a stare.

Captain on leave, a lean dark mackerel
lies in the offing, turns himself and looks
through currents of sound. The flat-eyed flatfish
sucks on a straw, staring from its repose, laxly.

And gallants in shoals swim up and lag
circling and passing near the white attraction;
sometimes pausing, opening a conversation:
fish pause so to nibble or tug.

But now the ice-cream is finished, is
paid for. The fish swim off on business
and she sits alone at the table, a white stone
useless except to a collector, a rich man.

KEITH DOUGLAS

14

(ii) Thinking about a poem's images

Writers and readers are both dealers in images. It is often through images that we get new insights into the world and fresh ways of looking at things. Usually this means seeing a likeness where we have previously seen only difference. So, when a poet describes bats 'like bits of umbrella' we see why he makes the comparison and can see the dark, stretched membrane of skin between the fragile bones. Neither bats, nor umbrellas, will be quite the same again! This is the poet making a new image from putting together two quite ordinary things. In this way a great deal may be said in a very short space. Samuel Beckett in his play *Waiting for Godot* writes

> They give birth astride of a grave, the light
> gleams an instant, then it's night once more.

Few lines will give such a terrifyingly stark image of human life; many poems may contain lines that are just playful or unusual ways of looking. Sometimes it may take a minute or two for the picture to come clear in your mind—rather like a photograph in the developing dish.

It is useful in these few minutes to make your own jottings, simply noting down in a phrase what the words make you see in your mind's eye, or identifying puzzling bits. It is best if you can work on a copy of a poem, underlining and adding your notes around the words, so that you build up a picture of your own 'reading'. Try it with the following poem. We have started with some notes to give you the idea. Carry on by yourself before sharing your thoughts with other members of the class.

The Window Cleaner

4 sided court enclosed
by buildings —
hundreds of windows

good image —
bumpy, black
surface

The college quad is cobbled like a blackberry
and shining in the rain and dangerous . . .

window-
cleaning
in the rain?

The window cleaner cups a telescopic caber—
Blondin never trod so warily.

Who's he?

He wears a sad expression on his face,
half a dress, and heather-mixture trews—

all day he listens to the squeak of puppies,
litters he is paid to drown and strangle.

All day he sees himself in the glass darkly
and waves goodbye, goodbye, goodbye.

All day he wrings his hands, crying buckets.
He'd rather shave shop windows clean

than climb this bendy Jacob's ladder
and risk the washboard fall of seraphim . . .

CRAIG RAINE

(iii) Ideas into images

A different use of imagery can be seen in this poem by George Herbert, a seventeenth-century writer who was a parish priest:

The Church-Floore

Mark you the floore? that square and speckled stone,
　　　Which looks so firm and strong,
　　　　　Is *Patience*:

And th'other black and grave, wherewith each one
　　　Is checker'd all along,
　　　　　Humilitie:

The gentle rising, which on either hand
　　　Leads to the Quire above,
　　　　　Is *Confidence*:

But the sweet cement, which in one sure band
　　　Ties the whole frame, is *Love*
　　　　　And *Charitie*.

Hither sometimes Sinne steals, and stains
The marble's neat and curious veins:
But all is cleansed when the marble weeps.
　　Sometimes Death, puffing at the doore,
　　Blows all the dust about the floore:
But while he thinks to spoil the room, he sweeps.
　　Blest be the *Architect*, whose art
　　Could build so strong in a weak heart.

You will see at once that the stones of the church floor stand for some of the different Christian virtues and that the poem is really a kind of parable where everything symbolises something. In pairs, talk about how these different qualities are represented and about the roles of the three characters, *Sinne*, *Death*, and the *Architect* who appear in the second part of the poem. Further work might include a poster illustrating the poem.

Some things can be made real and immediate only through the use of images. Abstract ideas are often communicated in this way as

the next two poems show. Read *Days* through to yourself and then
hear it read aloud, perhaps by three voices each taking a *sentence* in
turn.

Days

They come to us
Empty but not clean—
Like unrinsed bottles

Sides clouded
With a film
Of yesterday.

We can't keep them.
Our task is to fill up
And return.

There are no wages.
The reward is said to be
The work itself.

And if we question this,
Get angry, scream
At their round clock faces

Or try to break the glass,
We only hurt ourselves.
The days remain intact.

They wake us up
With light and leave us
In the dark.

For night is not
Their weakness—but a tease
To make us dream of death.

There is no end to days.
Only a cloth laid
Over a birdcage.

VICKI FEAVER

Milk bottles, clock faces, covering a birdcage . . . What thoughts do these images carry in the poem?

It *is* difficult to grasp the abstract. It might be worth discussing how you visualise, for example, God, heaven, hell, time, death. Perhaps you could write a poem around your own mental images of these; one possible starting point might be to look at the picture opposite. Its title is *The Healer*. Why do you think the painter called it this? How do you react to what you see?

Read the second poem on pp. 20–1 through to yourself two or three times and ask yourself what are the ideas and images here. As before, if you can use a copy, you will find that it helps to *underline* the main ideas and to make *jottings* around the poem about the images you see and any problem bits you find. When you have worked on the poem alone for five or ten minutes, share your ideas and images with the rest of the class.

© ADAGP, Paris and DACS, London, 1988: *The Healer* by Rene Magritte (1937)

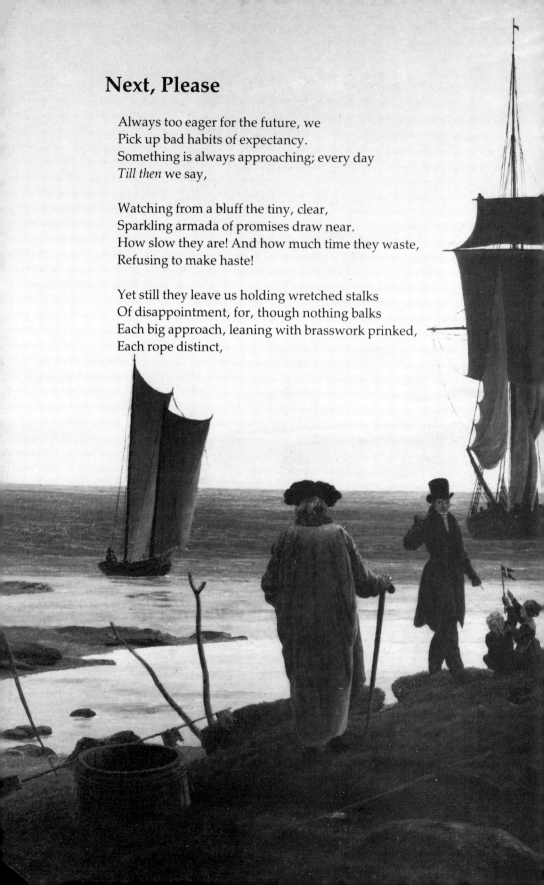

Next, Please

Always too eager for the future, we
Pick up bad habits of expectancy.
Something is always approaching; every day
Till then we say,

Watching from a bluff the tiny, clear,
Sparkling armada of promises draw near.
How slow they are! And how much time they waste,
Refusing to make haste!

Yet still they leave us holding wretched stalks
Of disappointment, for, though nothing balks
Each big approach, leaning with brasswork prinked,
Each rope distinct,

Flagged, and the figurehead with golden tits
Arching our way, it never anchors; it's
No sooner present than it turns to past.
Right to the last

We think each one will heave to and unload
All good into our lives, all we are owed
For waiting so devoutly and so long.
But we are wrong:

Only one ship is seeking us, a black-
Sailed unfamiliar, towing at her back
A huge and birdless silence. In her wake
No waters breed or break.

PHILIP LARKIN

(iv) Feelings into images

We have all felt longing, dislike, joy, fear and a whole range of other emotions at one time or another; yet, when we try to talk or write about our feelings the words often seem inadequate. To overcome this, some poems go straight on to the attack, insisting on our attention, or capturing us with their rhythms. Read the next two poems aloud.

Hey There Now!

(for Lesley)

Hey there now
my brownwater flower
     my sunchild branching
from my mountain river
     hey there now!
my young stream
       headlong
          rushing
I love to watch you
     when you're
    sleeping
      blushing

        GRACE NICHOLS

Dream Variation

To fling my arms wide
In some place of the sun,
To whirl and to dance
Till the white day is done.
Then rest at cool evening
Beneath a tall tree
While night comes on gently,
    Dark like me—
That is my dream!

To fling my arms wide
In the face of the sun,
Dance! whirl! whirl!
Till the quick day is done
Rest at pale evening . . .
A tall, slim tree . . .
Night coming tenderly,
    Black like me.

LANGSTON HUGHES

—What feelings do these poems express?
—What pictures do the words create as you read them?

Other images almost develop a life of their own. In some poems it may be difficult to pin down a precise meaning. You will probably be aware of songs where groups of images are used to create a mood or feeling, but where a *precise* meaning is hard to find—even unnecessary.

We are not suggesting that the poem which follows has no meaning—it has—but it is perhaps more a meaning that is *felt* through the strange nightmare image of the crabs than a meaning which is spelled out clearly. Hear the poem read aloud. Spend a few minutes jotting down what you saw in your mind's eye as the images developed. Then compare your ideas with those of other members of the class.

Ghost Crabs

At nightfall, as the sea darkens,
A depth darkness thickens, mustering from the gulfs and the
    submarine badlands,
To the sea's edge. To begin with
It looks like rocks uncovering, mangling their pallor.
Gradually the labouring of the tide
Falls back from its productions,
Its power slips back from glistening nacelles,*
    and they are crabs.
Giant crabs, under flat skulls, staring inland
Like a packed trench of helmets.

Ghosts, they are ghost-crabs.
They emerge
An invisible disgorging of the sea's cold
Over the man who strolls along the sands.
They spill inland, into the smoking purple
Of our woods and towns—a bristling surge
Of tall and staggering spectres
Gliding like shocks through water.
Our walls, our bodies, are no problem to them.
Their hungers are homing elsewhere.
We cannot see them or turn our minds from them.
Their bubbling mouths, their eyes
In a slow mineral fury
Press through our nothingness where we sprawl on our beds,
Or sit in our rooms. Our dreams are ruffled maybe.
Or we jerk awake to the world of our possessions
With a gasp, in a sweat burst, brains jamming blind
Into the bulb-light. Sometimes, for minutes, a sliding
Staring
Thickness of silence
Presses between us. These crabs own this world.
All night, around us or through us,
They stalk each other, they fasten on to each other,
They mount each other, they tear each other to pieces,
They utterly exhaust each other.
They are the powers of this world.
We are their bacteria,
Dying their lives and living their deaths.
At dawn, they sidle back under the sea's edge.
They are the turmoil of history, the convulsion
In the roots of blood, in the cycles of concurrence.
To them, our cluttered countries are empty battleground.
All day they recuperate under the sea.
Their singing is like a thin sea-wind flexing in the rocks of a
    headland,
Where only crabs listen.

They are God's only toys.

TED HUGHES

* outer casing of an aeroplane's engine

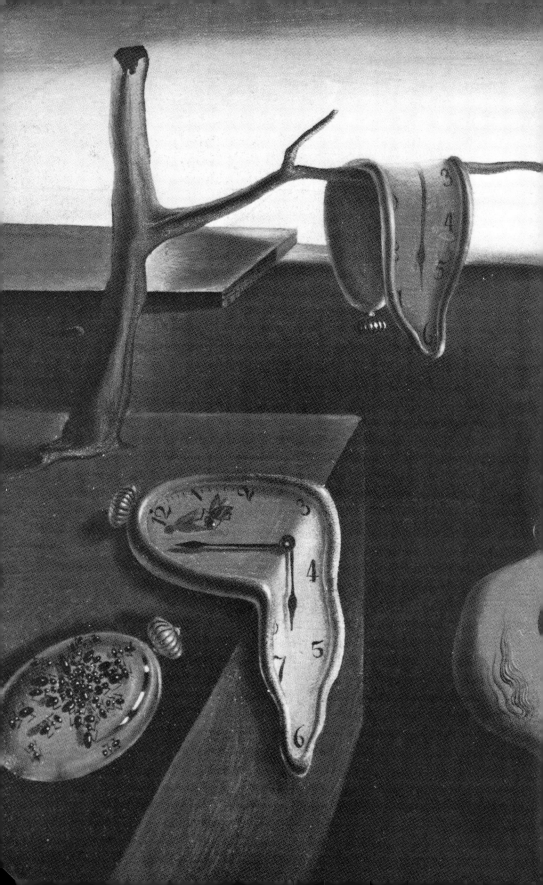

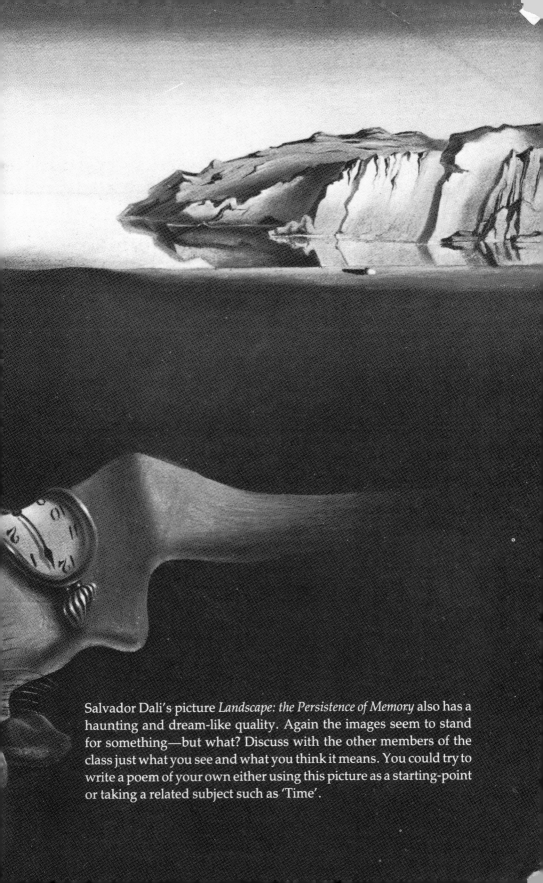

Salvador Dali's picture *Landscape: the Persistence of Memory* also has a haunting and dream-like quality. Again the images seem to stand for something—but what? Discuss with the other members of the class just what you see and what you think it means. You could try to write a poem of your own either using this picture as a starting-point or taking a related subject such as 'Time'.

Forms

If you flick through the pages of this collection of poems one of the first things that tells you it *is* a collection of poems and not, say, of short stories or a novel is that there are many short pieces which have very different shapes on the page. There are poems divided into neat four line verses and poems that straggle down the page with no recognisable shape or pattern; there are chunky fourteen line poems and sharp little two-liners; some poems are composed entirely of long lines and others of short ones. To look at them they are often very different but they are, as their *form* on the page tells you, all of them poems of one sort or another.

If you begin to read aloud or listen to the poems in your head you quickly find that many of the lines *rhyme* with each other. Some lines rhyme in pairs at the end of the line; some lines rhyme words in the middle of the line with words at the end of the same line and there are all sorts of other variations in the pattern of rhyming.

As you read aloud you can't help noticing that many poems have a clearly defined *rhythm*, a pattern of strong and light stresses to the words that makes you say them in a particular way.

Writers choose particular forms of poem, particular shapes on the page, and they choose rhyme schemes and rhythmic patterns quite deliberately. It is a skilled craft to bring all these technical elements together in a way that helps the writer to say what he or she feels and to communicate successfully with unknown readers.

In this section we shall be looking at some of the verse forms that writers use. It's helpful to start by looking at two aspects of poetry that we've already noticed: rhyme and rhythm. We hope you will not mind too much if, to do so, we go back first of all to a time when you were very much younger . . .

(i) Rhyme

Humpty Dumpty sat on a wall
Humpty Dumpty had a great fall . . .

Mary, Mary quite contrary
How does your garden grow?
With silver bells and cockle shells
And pretty maids all in a row.

Remember these? Quickly jot down any lines from nursery rhymes you remember from when you were much younger. Spend no more than two or three minutes on the task. Now share your ideas with your neighbour and with the class.

Almost certainly most of your examples will have strong rhyme patterns. Some of them will be very simple as in *Humpty Dumpty*; some will be more complicated as in *Mary, Mary*. Ring around the rhyme words in your own examples. In *Mary, Mary* you have examples of what are called *end rhymes* and of *internal rhymes*. Internal rhymes are rhymes that occur inside a single line; end rhymes are, as their name suggests, words that rhyme at the very ends of lines. Can you say which are which?

Here is another example you may remember:

Doctor Foster went to Gloucester
In a shower of rain;
He stepped in a puddle, right up to his middle
And never went there again.

There are three sorts of rhyme here:

—Which are end rhymes?
—Which are internal rhymes?
—Although most of the rhymes are *full rhymes*, one pair of rhymes is what is known as a *half rhyme*, that is a rhyme which although it sounds close, isn't a perfect match. Can you say which pair this is?

Now look back at your own examples of rhymes that you remembered and jotted down earlier. In pairs, decide which are full rhymes and which are half rhymes.

It is through nursery rhymes that most of us first hear rhymed verse and small children usually find them very pleasing and satisfying. If you have younger brothers or sisters at the nursery rhyme stage you will find that they enjoy supplying the rhyming words if you pause before the rhyme word:

'Jack Sprat could eat no . . . ?
'Little Polly Flinders / Sat among the . . . ?
'Old Mother Hubbard / Went to the . . . ?

The predictability of the rhyme and the security of knowing what comes next contribute a good deal to this enjoyment and it certainly helps us remember the lines. Think how long it is since anyone asked you to remember a nursery rhyme; yet it's fairly certain that, once a line had been triggered in your memory, the rest of the rhyme came flooding back although you had not thought of it for years.

Advertisers know about and use the power of rhymes to stay in our memories. You can probably think of television adverts that rely on rhyming jingles.

—In pairs, quickly jot down any examples of rhymed advertisements that you can remember. Compare your list with others in the class. Do any of the rhymes date back several years?

Human beings seem to like rhyme from the first time they meet it as babies and young children. We go on developing our feeling for rhyme through playground rhymes and chants, limericks, poems and songs that we play over and over again. Rhyme is important in all of these whether it is bold and strong as in the nursery rhymes or more subtle and complex as in many poems and songs. It is almost always there, acting as a kind of 'cement' which helps to bind the words together, helps them flow, creates a mood or a feeling, and helps them live in our memories.

A human skeleton in a museum prompted one writer to produce the poem opposite. It's clever and depends on its perky rhyme to create a certain mood.

The next poem (on page 32) also uses the same *rhyme scheme* where the second and fourth lines rhyme in each verse, abcb, but the sense 'spills over' from line to line.

To A Human Skeleton
(Encountered in the Museum of Natural History)

It's hard to think,
Albeit true,
That without flesh
I'd be like you.

And harder still
To think, old pal,
That one of these
Fine days I shall.

RICHARD ARMOUR

The Grey Squirrel

Like a small grey
coffee-pot
sits the squirrel.
He is not

all he should be,
kills by dozens
trees, and eats
his red-brown cousins.

The keeper on the
other hand,
who shot him, is
a Christian, and

loves his enemies.
Which shows
the squirrel was not
one of those.

HUMBERT WOLFE

Rhyme can give a sharp edge to a poem – sometimes a cutting edge deliberately chosen to hurt. Alexander Pope, a poet who wrote about two hundred and fifty years ago, perfected the art of the wounding *rhymed couplet* where the lines are rhymed in pairs. Here he is attacking his enemy, Lord Hervey, who has been described as 'a miminy-piminy official' at the royal court of the time, a man who was 'all airs and graces and intrigue, a sort of neuter . . .'

> Yet let me flap this bug with gilded wings,
> This painted child of dirt, that stinks and stings;
> Whose buzz the witty and the fair annoys,
> Yet wit ne'er tastes, and beauty ne'er enjoys:
> So well-bred spaniels civilly delight
> In mumbling of the game they dare not bite.
> Eternal smiles his emptiness betray,
> As shallow streams run dimpling all the way.

He continues for a further fifteen poisonous lines describing Hervey as a 'familiar toad' who

> Half froth, half venom, spits himself abroad,
> In puns, or politics, or tales, or lies,
> Or spite, or smut, or rhymes, or blasphemies . . .

until he finally demolishes his adversary with the contemptuous couplet

> Beauty that shocks you, parts that none will trust,
> Wit that can creep, and pride that licks the dust.

Pope was a master of the short, sharp, cleverly worded poems which are called *epigrams*. Here is one that he wrote and had engraved on the collar of one of the royal dogs at Kew palace. Imagine yourself bending down to see what was written there and reading:

> I am his Highness' dog at Kew;
> Pray tell me sir, whose dog are you?

It's rather like being poked in the eye with a sharp stick!

—Using this poem as a model, try writing an epigram of your own—lines to be found by somebody looking in your bag or a couplet to go in the back window of a car, basing it on the familiar stickers which say things like 'I may be slow but I'm in front of you' and so on.

The Russian writer Mayakovsky saw rhyme as potentially dangerous stuff.

As we poets see it,
                        a barrel the rhyme is,
          a barrel of dynamite,
                    the fuse is
                                each line.
          The line starts smoking,
                        exploding the line is,
          and the stanza
                    blows
                    a city
                        sky-high.

Perhaps he seems to be claiming too much, but don't forget the
many writers who have been silenced because their rhymes wound
those in power or that the voice of protest is often heard most
forcefully in a song. (Even *Humpty Dumpty*, *Mary*, *Mary*, and *Doctor
Foster* referred to people and political events of their day: some think
Mary was Mary, Queen of Scots who was imprisoned by her sister
Queen Elizabeth I.)

Not all rhyme is sharply pointed or barbed in the way we have
seen so far. Many poets use rhyme in an altogether quieter, more
restrained way as something that helps give the poem shape and
holds it together.

Wilfred Owen, who later became perhaps the best known poet of
the First World War, wrote this tranquil piece when he was a young
man living in France some time before the outbreak of hostilities.
Notice how he uses both rhyme and half-rhyme as a way of giving
the poem a structure. The half rhymes are at the beginning of each
line; the full rhymes at the end.

From My Diary, July 1914

Leaves
   Murmuring by myriads in the shimmering trees.
Lives
   Wakening with wonder in the Pyrenees.
Birds
   Cheerily chirping in the early day.
Bards
   Singing of summer, scything thro' the hay.
Bees
   Shaking the heavy dews from bloom and frond.
Boys
   Bursting the surface of the ebony pond.
Flashes
   Of swimmers carving thro' the sparkling cold.
Fleshes
   Gleaming with wetness to the morning gold.
A mead
   Bordered about with warbling water brooks.
A maid
   Laughing the love-laugh with me; proud of looks.
The heat
   Throbbing between the upland and the peak.
Her heart
   Quivering with passion to my pressed cheek.
Braiding
   Of floating flames across the mountain brow.
Brooding
   Of stillness; and a sighing of the bough.
Stirs
   Of leaflets in the gloom; soft petal-showers;
Stars
   Expanding with the starr'd nocturnal flowers.

WILFRED OWEN

Rhyme is used quite consciously—maybe a shade too self-consciously—to create a mood. The single words that begin each line, the jottings from his diary, are gently held together by the device of half-rhyme.

The poem moves through the day, beginning with wakening to the early day, moving through the freshness of the morning, the heat of the afternoon sun, and ending in the soft gloom of evening with the stars opening.

—Try to write a poem in the same pattern yourself using the pairs of half rhymes and full rhymes. What you are aiming for is a set of loosely-linked word-pictures. You may find it helpful to do as Owen does and, once you have chosen your subject, to develop it over a fixed period of time. There are innumerable topics you could approach in this way: your own day, from waking to going to bed; the seasons of the year or days of the week; growing up from babyhood to old age; an activity such as a football match, from the crowds converging on the stadium, through the various incidents of the game, to the empty stands when it is all over. Almost everything has a pattern you could use. Sharing your ideas with a partner and working in pairs may help.

(ii) Rhythm and Metre

In the previous section we noted that people seemed to get a lot of pleasure from rhymes and looked at examples of nursery rhymes that very young children enjoy. Of course, it isn't only the rhyme that makes them so lively and memorable: the rhythm helps too. Most nursery rhymes have a very marked rhythmic pattern of strong and light stresses. We can show the pattern by marking / for syllables with a strong stress and x for those with a light one or with no stress at all:

    / x   / x   /   x   / x
Mary, Mary quite contrary

—Now copy out the line below and mark the stresses:

Doctor Foster went to Gloucester

Don't forget that Gloucester is pronounced 'Gloster' and so has only two syllables, not three.

There is a satisfying bouncy beat to the lines that children love. John Betjeman uses a similar bouncy rhythm in his poem *In Westminster Abbey* which you will find printed in full on page 147. A rather selfish lady is offering up her prayers during the last war:

Gracious Lord, Oh bomb the Germans
　　Spare their women for Thy sake
And if that is not too easy
　　We will pardon Thy mistake.

The dancing rhythm is ideal for poking fun at the lady's prayer and
puncturing any idea of seriousness we may be tempted to give it.
The rhythm of a poem is deliberately chosen by the writer to fit the
writer's mood and feelings towards the subject and it may suggest to
us a particular way of reading the poem.

　　Underlying many poems there is that almost mechanical pattern
of strong and light stresses which we call *metre* and which we have
already seen at work in the examples given above. Even single
words may have a natural stress pattern. Try these:

　　/　　x
Monday has a heavy stress followed by a light one;

　　x　/
Today works the other way round.

　　x　/　x
Tomorrow has a stressed syllable between two unstressed ones.

If you aren't sure about this, try reversing the stress patterns of
'Monday' and 'Today': it just isn't natural!

—In pairs, try saying a few other words yourself. Write down the
names of some of the people in your group e.g. David, Alison,
Christopher, Helen, Rebecca, Stephen and mark the stressed and
unstressed syllables in each one. Like this:

　/　x　　　　/　x　　x
David　　Alison

You may not always agree on the pattern: try the names over several
times stressing them differently before you decide.

　　The stresses in individual words can be fitted together into longer
groups within a line of verse. We are not going to look at all the
patterns and variations that writers use but it may be helpful to point
out the commonest and perhaps simplest one which is called *iambic
metre*. Here the writer takes the simple light/heavy pattern (x/) and
uses it as the basic rhythm of the line. If it is repeated five times in a
line—exactly the same pattern you would get if you said the word
'again' five times—then it is known as an *iambic pentameter*. (The x/
stress unit is properly known as an *iambus* or an *iambic foot* and

'penta' means 'five' just as it does in words like 'pentagon' meaning 'five-sided'.)

Rupert Brooke's poem *The Soldier* on page 177 uses iambic pentameters throughout:

on page 177

```
  x /  x      /  x   / x /   x  /
If I should die think only this of me
```

In fact, although this is the basic rhythm of the piece you will find some variations and discover that it doesn't thump along quite so predictably all the way through. These small irregularities help to keep the poem from being rather monotonous and add to its life and interest, although the overall pattern is that given above with five iambic feet and ten syllables to each line.

—Copy out this couplet by Robert Frost and write down the stress pattern above each line:

Forgive, O Lord

Forgive, O Lord, my little jokes on Thee,
And I'll forgive thy great big one on me.

The iambic metre is perhaps the closest rhythm to that of everyday speech and many writers in the past, particularly Shakespeare, used it when they were writing plays in verse. After a little practice you will probably find that it's quite easy to write fairly basic iambic verse . . .

Now try to write a line or two yourself
Whose patterns are the same as those you've seen.
In pairs, and with your English teacher's help,
You'll quickly see just what it is we mean!

How boring an unvaried and mechanically repeated rhythm becomes is very clear from the four lines of doggerel given above!

—In pairs, try to construct a set of instructions for a particular task in the way we have just done. How would you make a cup of tea in iambic pentameters? What might some washing instructions or a shopping list sound like?

Don't expect that many of the poems in this collection will fall into neat, regular rhythmic patterns. You will find a great many variations on the basic rhythms—variations that reflect changes in feeling, pace or attitude as the poem develops. The metre is often a sort of backing against which the writer composes a variety of melodies.

In the next poem, by the Caribbean poet John Agard (above), we see a striking example of the way in which a number of elements—the rhythm of the limbo dance, the sound and the fluid movement of the dancer bending ever lower to pass beneath the limbo stick, and a visual picture of that movement in the way the words are printed on the page—can be made to combine. Rhyme, rhythm and movement may seem to be entirely free but they are in fact carefully controlled.

Limbo Dancer's Soundpoem

Go
down
low
    low
        low

show
dem
what
you know
      know
          know

let
limb
flow
    flow
        flow

as sound
of drum
grow
    grow
      grow

& body
bend
like bow
    bow
      bow
        limb/bow
          low
            low
              low
                limb/bow

JOHN AGARD

(iii) Forms

Free Verse

There are many poems that have no formal metre at all yet still have the appearance and feel of verse. Look at the next poem.

Flight of the Roller Coaster

Once more around should do it, the man confided . . .

And sure enough, when the roller-coaster reached the peak
Of the giant curve above me—screech of its wheels
Almost drowned by the shriller cries of the riders—

Instead of the dip and plunge with its landslide of screams
It rose in the air like a movieland magic carpet, some wonderful
    bird,

And without fuss or fanfare swooped slowly across the
    amusement park,
Over Spook's Castle, ice-cream booths, shooting-gallery; and
    losing no height

Made the last yards above the beach, where the cucumber-cool
Brakeman in the last seat saluted
A lady about to change from her bathing-suit.

Then, as many witnesses duly reported, headed leisurely over
    the water,
Disappearing mysteriously all too soon behind a low-lying flight
    of clouds.

RAYMOND SOUSTER

Poems written in this way are *free verse*. Modern poets often use free verse and you will find many examples in this collection. The words of a free verse poem are not organised into a symmetrical pattern with a regular metre and a rhyme scheme, yet it would be wrong to think of this kind of verse as being formless. Some of it certainly is but in good free verse the shape and structure of the poem reflect the mood and meaning of the writer; the organisation of the poem arises directly out of what the poet wants to say. D. H. Lawrence was probably one of the most skilful writers of free verse. You may well have come across some of his animal poems already—*Bat*, *Mosquito*, *Mountain Lion* and *Snake* are some of the best known. Here is the opening of another of his animal poems, *Baby Tortoise*.

You know what it is to be born alone,
Baby tortoise!

The first day to heave your feet little by little from the shell,
Not yet awake,
And remain lapsed on earth,
Not quite alive.

A tiny, fragile, half-animate bean.
To open your tiny beak-mouth, that looks as if it would never
    open,
Like some iron door;
To lift the upper hawk-beak from the lower base
And reach your skinny little neck
And take your first bite at some dim bit of herbage,
Alone, small insect,
Tiny bright-eye,
Slow one,
To take your first solitary bite
And move on your slow, solitary hunt.
Your bright, dark little eye,
Your eye of a dark disturbed night,
Under its slow lid, tiny baby tortoise,
So indomitable.

—Which is the longest line, and which is the shortest?
—Which is the longest sentence and which is the shortest?
—Which words occur more than once at the beginning of lines?
—Why do you think the description is split up into two short sections and then a long one?
—Does the way the lines are arranged on the page make any difference to the way the poem reads? Would it be the same if it were printed as a solid block of prose?

You may well have written some free verse poems of your own already, but now that you have had the opportunity to discuss this form more fully try it again.

—Choose your own subject. If you would like an idea to start you off, you could try continuing Raymond Souster's poem yourself: where did the roller coaster go after it disappeared behind the bank of cloud? Or try writing your own animal description with the same kind of intense attention to detail that D. H. Lawrence shows in his poem.
—Remember: don't worry about rhyme or regular metre. Try the lines over to yourself in your head and choose line lengths that suit what it is you are trying to say; leave out any words that are not earning their keep; try for a piece that isn't simply chopped up prose.
—Work over your first version with these ideas in mind until you feel it says what you want it to say in the most economical way possible. Don't be afraid to ask for advice.

Rhyming Couplets

We have already met the idea of pairs of lines that rhyme. *Humpty Dumpty,* Pope's description of Lord Hervey, Frost's little poem *Forgive, O Lord* all have such rhymed pairs of lines or *rhymed couplets* as they are known. They seem simple enough to construct but it's difficult to develop a piece entirely in rhymed couplets without becoming very repetitive and letting the rhyme take over. Pope knew this and complained about writers who allowed obvious rhymes to take over the sense of the poem:

Where'er you find 'the cooling western breeze,'
In the next line it 'whispers through the trees':
If crystal streams 'with pleasing murmurs creep,'
The reader's threatened, not in vain, with 'sleep'.

It takes a good deal of careful thought and experiment to write couplets that effortlessly say what you want:

> True ease in writing comes from art, not chance,
> As those move easiest who have learned to dance.

Still, we all have to start somewhere and there is no better way of understanding the degree of skill needed than that of trying to write your own rhymed couplets. If all this seems too serious, don't forget that the first four lines of any *limerick*—a form you have probably known about for years—are made up of two rhymed couplets:

> There was an old man with a beard
> Who said "It is just as I feared!—
>> Two Owls and a Hen,
>> Four Larks and a Wren,
> Have all built their nests in my beard."

The *Clerihew*, invented by Edward Clerihew Bentley, is just two rhymed couplets with lines of irregular length:

> Edward the Confessor
> Slept under the dresser.
> When that began to pall
> He slept in the hall.

You should find it not too difficult to write rhymed couplets: in fact, once you get the knack, it can be quite fun.

—Try your hand at producing a piece that depends on rhymed couplets for some of its effect. You could tackle the basic Clerihew or the limerick or the more demanding rhymed couplet of the type that Alexander Pope often used. If you take up the last suggestion notice that there are usually ten syllables to be heard in each line.
—Remember: try not to let the rhyme take over the meaning so completely that what you write becomes artificial, awkward, or even totally meaningless; try not to produce more rhyme than reason.

You may find it helps to write in pairs and if you have problems in arriving at a perfect couplet, don't despair but remember Pope's remark:

> Whoever thinks a faultless piece to see
> Thinks what ne'er was, nor is, nor e'er shall be.

Now you know why poets often used to use the poetic form 'ne'er' instead of writing 'never' and 'e'er' instead of 'ever': it allowed them to cheat a little and use one syllable instead of two. That's how Pope manages to keep that second line down to ten syllables and maintain the metrical pattern.

Ballad

The *ballad* form is very ancient and seems to be one of the most natural of metrical forms for English poetry. What it does is to tell a story. The early ballads were not simply read but were often sung to a group of people and sometimes the singer would accompany himself on a harp. The singers of medieval times chose the ballad form for their stories of fighting and love, their tales of mystery and the supernatural just as, in more recent times, writers have used and continue to use the ballad in work songs and in hundreds of stories of lovers set to music in song lyrics. It's a fair bet that in this week's Top Forty there will be a few ballads: the ballad form is a survivor!

We have chosen a modern ballad written in the style of one of the medieval ballads to illustrate the form:

Lord Lovelace

Lord Lovelace rode home from the wars,
　　His wounds were black as ice,
While overhead the winter sun
　　Hung out its pale device.

The lance was tattered in his hand,
　　Sundered his axe and blade,
And in a bloody coat of war
　　Lord Lovelace was arrayed.

And he was sick and he was sore
　　But never sad was he,
And whistled bright as any bird
　　Upon an April tree.

'Soon, soon,' he cried, 'at Lovelace Hall
　　Fair Ellen I shall greet,
And she with loving heart and hand
　　Will make my sharp wounds sweet.

45

'And Young Jehan the serving-man
   Will bring the wine and bread,
And with a yellow link will light
   Us to the bridal bed.'

But when he got to Lovelace Hall
   Burned were both wall and stack,
And in the stinking moat the tower
   Had tumbled on its back.

And none welcomed Lord Lovelace home
   Within the castle shell,
And ravaged was the land about
   That Lord Lovelace knew well.

Long in his stirrups Lovelace stood
   Before his broken door,
And slowly rode he down the hill
   Back to the bitter war.

Nor mercy showed he from that day,
   Nor tear fell from his eye,
And rich and poor both fearful were
   When Black Lovelace rode by.

This tale is true that now I tell
   To woman and to man,
As Fair Ellen is my wife's name
   And mine is Young Jehan.

CHARLES CAUSLEY

Working in pairs, discuss:

—What has happened in the story?

—Notice how the tale is told very economically. The writer concentrates on a few key scenes (vss 1–3; vss 4–5; vss 6–8; vss 9–10): what happens in each?

—What is the rhyme scheme for each verse?

—What is the metrical pattern of the verses? How many stresses are there in each line?

There are many variations in the ballad form but it is basically four lines rhymed either *abab*, or *abcb*, with a 4,3,4,3, stress pattern. That may sound complicated but simply listen to the poem being read, try it on the ear and you will find it is not too difficult to master.

—Try to write a ballad of your own. You will find it helps to focus you on the story if you choose and name a central character from the outset: somebody real whom you know, somebody in the news, somebody out of the past, somebody you have imagined . . . One class, instead of choosing a single character, decided to write *The Ballad of 4B* and celebrated the (often quite unbelievable) talents of the class in a ballad of thirty verses which they all worked on together with everybody contributing a few lines.

—Once you have written your ballad, you may be able to give it some sort of musical accompaniment, particularly if you or a friend can play guitar.

The Sonnet

The *sonnet* is a form which will make more demands on your ingenuity than any of the others. It is intricate but it is also very satisfying to succeed in creating one that works.

The first thing to realise is that this form gives the writer a precise framework for his or her ideas as it must be composed of fourteen lines, each one an iambic pentameter (look back to p. 37 to remind yourself of the metre). These two rules govern all sonnets, but the rhyme schemes vary according to which of the two types of sonnet the poet is writing. The *Italian* (or *Petrarchan*) sonnet consists of eight lines, called the *octave*, rhymed on two sounds and arranged as two four-line units, *abba abba*. In the remaining six lines, called the *sestet*, two or three new rhymes appear, often arranged as two three-line units, *ccd ccd* or *cde cde*, or, as in this poem, *Glasgow Sonnet*, by Edwin Morgan, *cdc dcd*.

Glasgow Sonnet

A mean wind wanders through the backcourt trash.
Hackles on puddles rise, old mattresses
puff briefly and subside. Play-fortresses
of brick and bric-a-brac spill out some ash.
Four storeys have no windows left to smash,
but in the fifth a chipped sill buttresses
mother and daughter the last mistresses
of that black block condemned to stand, not crash.
Around them the cracks deepen, the rats crawl.
The kettle whimpers on a crazy hob.
Roses of mould grow from ceiling to wall.
The man lies late since he has lost his job,
smokes on one elbow, letting his coughs fall
thinly into an air too poor to rob.

The *English* (or *Shakespearean*) type of sonnet is constructed in three four-line units and a couplet. The rhyme scheme, therefore, is usually *abab, cdcd, efef, gg*. Sometimes there is a shift in the thought of the poem between the octave and the sestet—as commonly happens in the Italian sonnet—but often the poet will smooth over this division and, instead, use the final couplet as a unifying and summarising point of the poem.

Shakespeare's sonnet, *My Mistress' Eyes*, was written partly as a reply to other writers of his day who produced fashionable but highly exaggerated sonnets in praise of the women (real or imagined) with whom they were in love. Shakespeare teases these poets and their ridiculous, overblown comparisons—'My Mistress' eyes are like the sun' was a fairly typical boast. He takes their usual list of similes—lips = red coral; white breast = snow; hair = fine gold wire; cheeks = roses; breath = perfume; voice = music; movement = like a goddess—and denies that his lady is anything like this. Of course, he cleverly turns his denials around in the last couplet where he claims that nonetheless his mistress is more beautiful than any of those who are falsely praised by the other poets.

Sonnet 130

My mistress' eyes are nothing like the sun;
Coral is far more red than her lips' red;
If snow be white, why then her breasts are dun;
If hairs be wires, black wires grow on her head.
I have seen roses damask'd, red and white,
But no such roses see I in her cheeks;
And in some perfumes there is more delight
Than in the breath that from my mistress reeks,
I love to hear her speak, yet well I know
That music hath a far more pleasing sound;
I grant I never saw a goddess go—
My mistress when she walks treads on the ground.
    And yet, by heaven, I think my love as rare
    As any she belied by false compare.

Sonnets generally require a fair amount of working and re-working before the writer is satisfied with them. In order to show how one writer grappled with the writing of a poem that has since become one of the best known sonnets in the language, we have printed on the following pages the first and last of Wilfred Owen's four drafts of *Anthem for Doomed Youth*. You may even notice that he sought out the help of another writer, Siegfried Sassoon, and that some of Sassoon's pencilled amendments are clearly visible.

—What differences do you notice between the first and last drafts?
—Compare the opening four lines of the two versions and try to account for some of the changes. Does Owen make alterations simply to change the meaning, or to create certain sound effects or particular rhythms?
—Do you agree with Owen's final decision about the title? Why might he prefer 'doomed' to 'dead'?

—Finally, having spent some time discussing Owen's poem and the other sonnets, try to write a poem in sonnet form yourself.

Anthem for Dead Youth.

What passing bells for these who die so fast?
  — Only the monstrous anger of our guns.
Let the majestic insults of their mouths
Be as the priest words of their burials.
Of choristers and holy music, none;
  Nor any voice of mourning, save the wail
The long-drawn wail of high far-sailing shells.

What candles may we hold for these lost souls?
  — Not in the hands of boys, but in their eyes
Shall many candles shine, and
And Women's wide-spreaded arms shall be their wreaths,
And pallor of girls cheeks shall be their palls.
Their flowers, the tenderness of minds,
And each slow Dusk, a drawing-down of blinds.

First Draft
(With Sassoon's amendments.)

Anthem for ~~Dead~~ Youth.

What passing-bells for ~~these~~ who die as cattle?
  — Only the monstrous anger of the guns.
  Only the stuttering rifles' rapid rattle
Can patter out their hasty orisons.
No {~~music for all them~~; ~~from~~} prayers ~~or~~ bells,
  Nor any voice of mourning save the choirs,
The shrill ~~demented~~ choirs of wailing shells;
  And bugles calling ~~sad across the~~ shires.
                   for them from sad

What candles may be held to speed them all?
  Not in the hands of boys, but in their eyes
Shall shine the holy glimmers of goodbyes.
~~And~~ The pallor of girls' brows shall be their pall;
  Their flowers the tenderness of {~~silent patient~~} minds,
And each slow dusk a drawing-down of blinds.

(Pencil words were written by
S.S. when W. showed him the
sonnet at Craiglockhart in
Sept. 1917.)

Fourth and final draft

51

Syllabic Verse is, as its name suggests, verse that is held together simply by having the same number of syllables in each line. It is a fairly easy, light structure and often has a conversational tone as in these opening lines of a poem about pigeons by Fiona Pitt-Kethley:

> I used to love to watch their delicate
> shades of grey as they swaggered on the lawn,
> jostling for bits of bread I'd left for them.

As you see, she has chosen to shape her poem by keeping to a ten syllable line.

Haiku is a Japanese form with which you may already be familiar. It too is based on the number of syllables in the line but they are arranged in a particular pattern to total seventeen syllables in all with five syllables in the first line, seven in the second and five in the third—like this:

Bamboo Grove

> Song of the cuckoo:
> In the grove of great bamboos,
> Moonlight seeping through.

BASHO

Of course, in translation from the Japanese, the number of syllables does not always work out perfectly! Although this translator has chosen to rhyme the first and third lines that is not in fact strictly necessary. It can be quite a challenge to structure your thoughts in seventeen syllables and at least one writer has taken the easy way out.

First Haiku of Spring

> cuck oo cuck oo cuck
> oo cuck oo cuck oo cuck oo
> cuck oo cuck oo cuck

ROGER McGOUGH

Tanka is another Japanese form which is based on syllable pattern. Like haiku it has three lines of five, seven, and five syllables but it continues for a further two lines, each of which has seven syllables.

A *Cinquain*, as its name suggests, has five lines. They are arranged on a syllabic pattern with two syllables in the first line, four in the second, six in the third, eight in the fourth and then back to two syllables in the fifth and last line: twenty-two syllables in all:

Mr Death at the Door

Butler,
Open up for
It is Mr Death come
To see how well I am doing.
How kind!

REBECCA BAZELEY

The forms described above do not generally rhyme but there are syllabic verse forms that combine both a set number of syllables to a line with a particular rhyme scheme. The *triolet* is one example of such a form and it usually has eight lines of eight syllables each, with the same lines reappearing. The first line recurs as the fourth and the seventh and the second recurs as the eighth line. Here, Wendy Cope uses the triolet structure though the syllable pattern is not a regular eight to a line.

Triolet

I used to think all poets were Byronic—
Mad, bad and dangerous to know.
And then I met a few. Yes it's ironic—
I used to think all poets were Byronic.
They're mostly wicked as a ginless tonic
And wild as pension plans. Not long ago
I used to think all poets were Byronic
Mad, bad and dangerous to know.

WENDY COPE

The writer of the next poem has gone even further. Can you work out a pattern to the syllables and the recurring lines? It's maddening but you will find that there is one. It is in fact a highly unusual form known as a *pantoum*:

Vase/Faces

To start with, you may realise
Two facing profiles, filled in black:
Like this. But is it otherwise?
They disappear and then are back:

Two facing profiles, filled in black,
Or should it be a jar of light?
They disappear and then are back.
The day is followed by the night.

Or should it be a jar of light?
It must be *this* or *that* you say.
The day is followed by the night,
But then the night precedes the day.

It must be *this* or *that* you say?
Why deal in terms like good and bad?
But then, the night precedes the day,
The two at once would drive you mad.

Why deal in terms like good and bad?
Why make a choice between the two?
The two at once would drive you mad,
That's all I have to say to you.

Why make a choice between the two?
Because we've done it all along;
That's all I have to say to you.
Of course, I could have got things wrong,

Because we've done it all along
Like this—but is it otherwise?
Of course, I could have got things wrong
To start with, you may realise.

COLIN ROWBOTHAM

The puzzle presented by the pair of faces looking at each other and then fading away to become the image of a vase is only one of several examples of the way we see objects. Here are two more similar images:

What do you see? They are both two-in-one pictures. Choose one of the pictures and try writing a couplet or short verse which captures both the images you see.

In many poems, getting the form to work is part of the writer's satisfaction; recognising what the form is and how well it works is part of the reader's pleasure. There are dozens of different forms that might be explored and we have had room to mention only a few of them here. As you see, they give an insight into the poet's craft, they are challenging to experiment with and they remind all of us that poetry is in some ways a game which does not always have to be taken too seriously.

Making Poems

(i) Writers making poems

In the previous two sections we have discussed images and forms
—images giving a mental picture of ideas or feelings, forms giving
them shape and definition. Now we want you to read and talk about
two poems in which the writers explore their job as artists and
where they show us images and forms working together. You can
find more poems on the same theme on pages 68–83.

Read the first poem to yourself and be sure that you understand
why it has this title and not simply 'The Fox'. Notice the situation. At
the beginning the poet is sitting at his table, thinking about writing,
gazing into the blackness of the night through the window. This
blackness seems itself to be an image of his own mental blankness
until the fox enters his mind's eye.

Now, hear the poem read aloud.

The Thought-Fox

I imagine this midnight moment's forest:
Something else is alive
Besides the clock's loneliness
And this blank page where my fingers move.

Through the window I see no star:
Something more near
Though deeper within darkness
Is entering the loneliness:

Cold, delicately as the dark snow,
A fox's nose touches twig, leaf;
Two eyes serve a movement, that now
And again now, and now, and now

Sets neat prints into the snow
Between trees, and warily a lame
Shadow lags by stump and in hollow
Of a body that is bold to come

Across clearings, an eye,
A widening deepening greenness,
Brilliantly, concentratedly,
Coming about its own business

Till, with a sudden sharp hot stink of fox
It enters the dark hole of the head.
The window is starless still; the clock ticks,
The page is printed.

TED HUGHES

A poem about making a poem. How do the images and the form work together here? To explore how the poem is made, try this:

—What do you 'see' when you read and hear the poem? Jot down your own impressions of both the actual world of the poet's study and the imagined world of the fox emerging from the forest. Which seems the more vivid and real?
—What do you notice about the form of the poem? Note down anything that interests you about the rhymes, the four-line verses and the development of the poem. Talk about the poem and discuss your ideas with other members of your class.

When you are on your own away from the classroom you may be able to put yourself in a similar situation by clearing your mind of its immediate interests and focusing your attention on some feature-less object which can allow pictures to form in your imagination—a window, a sheet of paper in front of you, a wall. When an image forms itself, try to write down words, phrases, sense-impressions to capture this image as clearly as possible. From these notes you could develop your own piece of writing either as a prose description or a poem.

Here is another poet, seated by a window, preparing to write. Read it silently and then hear it read aloud.

Digging

Between my finger and my thumb
The squat pen rests; snug as a gun.

Under my window, a clean rasping sound
When the spade sinks into gravelly ground:
My father, digging. I look down

Till his straining rump among the flowerbeds
Bends low, comes up twenty years away
Stooping in rhythm through potato drills
Where he was digging.

The coarse boot nestled on the lug, the shaft
Against the inside knee was levered firmly.
He rooted out tall tops, buried the bright edge deep
To scatter new potatoes that we picked
Loving their cool hardness in our hands.

By God, the old man could handle a spade.
Just like his old man.

My grandfather cut more turf in a day
Than any other man on Toner's bog.
Once I carried him milk in a bottle
Corked sloppily with paper. He straightened up
To drink it, then fell to right away

Nicking and slicing neatly, heaving sods
Over his shoulder, going down and down
For the good turf. Digging.

The cold smell of potato mould, the squelch and slap
Of soggy peat, the curt cuts of an edge
Through living roots awaken in my head.
But I've no spade to follow men like them.

Between my finger and my thumb
The squat pen rests
I'll dig with it.

SEAMUS HEANEY

This poem is built around a memory—a strong visual recollection from the writer's childhood. The poet's attention is taken away from his writing by hearing his father digging beneath his window.

Working in pairs, decide what you think about the following questions before sharing your ideas with the rest of the class:

—What mental pictures develop as the writer thinks about his father and grandfather twenty years earlier?
—What thoughts cross his mind about their work and his?
—Clearly, this poem does not have such a regular form as the previous one. What decides the shape of the verses?

All of us can remember people, incidents, moments of happiness, sadness or fear from our early years. If there is a particular memory of this sort which you recall vividly, you may be able to write about it as Seamus Heaney has done.

(ii) Readers making poems

Every reading of a poem is a different 'performance', whether we read it ourselves or hear someone else do so. It is rather like hearing music we already know. We often find something new or different each time we listen. So it is with poems. The same words are in the same order on the page—they don't change any more than the notes in a musical score—but our performances change. Not only will there be different 'readings' from one person to the next, but there will be variations when we read a poem for a second or third time.

One way to discover how we read poems and to see this variety is to make some notes about your thoughts and feelings, starting in the same way that we described earlier with Craig Raine's *The Window Cleaner* (p. 16). This time, however, keep track of *how* you read by *numbering your notes around the poem* in the order in which you make them. Ideally, it is best to work on a copy of the poem.

Try the following sequence of activities with Brian Patten's poem *Frogs in the Wood* before comparing your 'readings' of the poem with the 'readings' of the three pupils which we have printed on pages 63–65.

Frogs in the Wood

How good it would be to be lost again,
Night falling on the compass and the map
Turning to improbable flames,
Bright ashes going out in the ponds.

And how good it would be
To stand bewildered in a strange wood
Where you are the loudest thing.
Your heart making a deafening noise.

And how strange when your fear of being lost has subsided
To stand listening to the frogs holding
Their arguments in the streams.
Condemning the barbarous herons.

And how right it is
To shrug off real and invented grief
As of no importance
To this moment of your life.

When being lost seems
So much more like being found,
And you find all that is lost
Is what weighed you down.

BRIAN PATTEN

Individually, carry out the following three steps:

—First, read the poem to yourself in the normal way. Note down
  how many times you read it before making your first jotting.
—Jot down your own responses to the poem, numbering them in
  sequence as you go. Your jottings might be about mental pictures
  you have during the reading, memories that the poem brings to
  mind, any puzzling bits, the overall feeling the poem gives you,
  and so on.

—Now, on a separate sheet, make a simple diagram of your 'readings' by ruling five horizontal lines (one for each of the five verses) and plotting the numbers on to your diagram in the appropriate places. Show by vertical lines how many times you read the poem before your first jotting. So, for example, if you read the poem through two-and-a-half times before making your first note about 'listening to the frogs' (vs. 3), followed by nine other jottings, then your diagram might look like this:

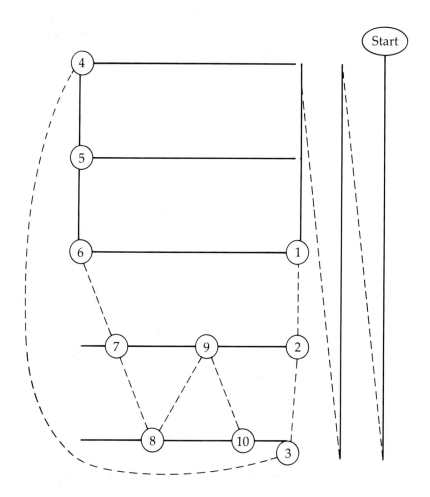

Use solid lines to represent continuous reading and responses, and broken lines to show where you jump from one part of the poem to another.

In groups, compare your 'readings'.

—What do your diagrams show about how you read the poem? Are there any bits that most of you have commented upon? Through comparing notes, do there seem to be any key lines or ideas which sum up the poem for you?

—Now, compare your 'readings' with these three by pupils of your own age.

(i) Kristina

Kristina's diagram looked like this. She made her first note as soon as she had read the first line, then read on to the end, returning to verse 2 for her second note, and so on.

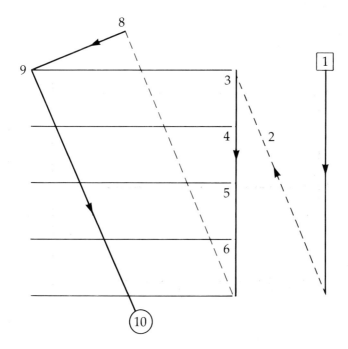

8. below you

1. childhood, lost child e.g. fairground
3. light falling, blurred eyesight, sunset
9. personal associations started memories of being frightened and isolated
2. frightened child/ animal
4. vivid memories of self as lost child
5. turns away from self and looks and listens around picture of frogs and streams and herons below viewpoint e.g. in a valley/dip in the land
6. loss
7. recall own memories and apply to self
10. this time memories of more recent incidents of childhood in earlier verses

63

(ii) Colin

Colin read the poem through completely three times before making his first note about the last line, jumping back to the first line and so on.

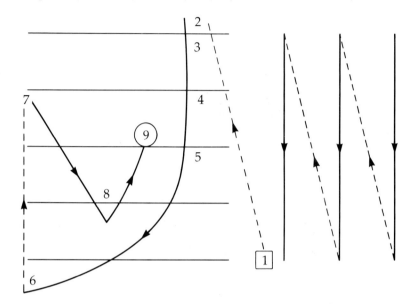

the middle of the poem reminded me of a week ago when I got lost with others in a wood. The responsibility of finding the way was no longer there

2. woods
3. water on fire like burning oil on water
4. you make the only noise amplified
7. dense undergrowth crashing through
9. life
5. looking around you
8. all worries gone

1. to lose something is not always a bad thing
6. relief at not having to find your way any more now that you are lost

(iii) Elizabeth

Elizabeth read the poem through very slowly once, making her first 7 or 8 notes in sequence, verse by verse, before jotting down a cluster of thoughts at the end (Nos 8–12). She then went back to the beginning again but not before she had made a longer note of a more personal nature shown in the boxed inset.

at the end, everywhere I've lived I've had my own private little place where I can be alone. Sometimes inside the house sometimes outside where I go to think or just to be alone – after first reading of the last verse.

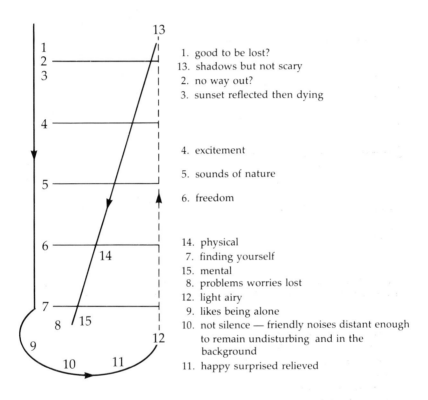

1. good to be lost?
13. shadows but not scary
2. no way out?
3. sunset reflected then dying

4. excitement

5. sounds of nature

6. freedom

14. physical
7. finding yourself
15. mental
8. problems worries lost
12. light airy
9. likes being alone
10. not silence — friendly noises distant enough to remain undisturbing and in the background
11. happy surprised relieved

Three very different ways of reading the same poem. *Your* 'readings' will be unique, too. Close attention like this is the reader's version of what the writer does when making a poem. As you can see by looking back at Wilfred Owen's drafts of *Anthem for Doomed Youth* (pp. 50–1), both poets and readers use jottings when making and re-making poems.

Try this sequence of activities with other poems. Once you are used to jotting down your responses in this way and comparing notes with others in your class (you don't have to do diagrams every time!) you will find your confidence in reading poetry greatly increases.

PART B

Anthology

Poets on Poetry

Leaving the Tate

Coming out with your clutch of postcards
in a Tate Gallery bag and another clutch
of images packed into your head you pause
on the steps to look across the river

and there's a new one: light bright buildings,
a streak of brown water, and such a sky
you wonder who painted it—Constable? No:
too brilliant. Crome? No: too ecstatic—

a madly pure Pre-Raphaelite sky,
perhaps, sheer blue apart from the white plumes
rushing up it (today, that is,
April. Another day would be different

but it wouldn't matter. All skies work.)
Cut to the lower right for a detail:
seagulls pecking on mud, below
two office blocks and a Georgian terrace.

Now swing to the left, and take in plane-trees
bobbled with seeds, and that brick building,
and a red bus . . . Cut it off just there,
by the lamp-post. Leave the scaffolding in.

That's your next one. Curious how
these outdoor pictures didn't exist
before you'd looked at the indoor pictures,
the ones on the walls. But here they are now,

marching out of their panorama
and queuing up for the viewfinder
your eye's become. You can isolate them
by holding your optic muscles still.

You can zoom in on figure studies
(that boy with the rucksack), or still lives,
abstracts, townscapes. No one made them.
The light painted them. You're in charge

of the hanging committee. Put what space
you like around the ones you fix on,
and gloat. Art multiplies itself.
Art's whatever you choose to frame.

FLEUR ADCOCK

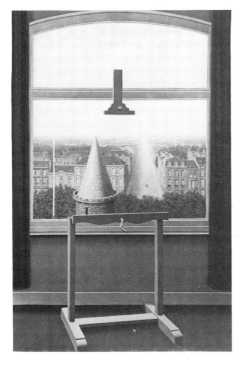

© ADAGP 1987: *Bather Between Light and Darkness* (1935) by Rene Magritte

Constantly Risking Absurdity

Constantly risking absurdity
                     and death
      whenever he performs
             above the heads
                  of his audience
    the poet like an acrobat
             climbs on rime
             to a high wire of his own making
  and balancing on eyebeams
               above a sea of faces
     paces his way
          to the other side of day
   performing entrechats
          and sleight-of-foot tricks
and other high theatrics
          and all without mistaking
     any thing
         for what it may not be

    For he's the super realist
              who must perforce perceive
    taut truth
        before the taking of each stance or
                      step
  in his supposed advance
          toward that still higher perch
where Beauty stands and waits
        with gravity
           to start her death-defying
                  leap

And he
   a little charleychaplin man
          who may or may not catch
   her fair eternal form
        spreadeagled in the empty air
  of existence

           LAWRENCE FERLINGHETTI

The Maker

So he said then: I will make the poem,
I will make it now. He took pencil,
The mind's cartridge, and blank paper,
And drilled his thoughts to the slow beat

Of the blood's drum; and there it formed
On the white surface and went marching
Onward through time, while the spent cities
And dry hearts smoked in its wake.

R. S. THOMAS

Jordan II

When first my lines of heaven'ly joyes made mention,
Such was their lustre, they did so excell,
That I sought out quaint words, and trim invention;
My thoughts began to burnish, sprout, and swell,
Curling with metaphors a plain intention,
Decking the sense, as if it were to sell.

Thousands of notions in my brain did runne,
Off'ring their service, if I were not sped:
I often blotted what I had begunne;
This was not quick enough, and that was dead.
Nothing could seem too rich to clothe the sunne,
Much lesse those joyes which trample on his head.

As flames do work and winde, when they ascend,
So did I weave myself into the sense.
But while I bustled, I might heare a friend
Whisper, *How wide is all this long pretence!*
There is in love a sweetnesse readie penn'd:
Copie out onely that, and save expense.

GEORGE HERBERT

71

Listen Mr Oxford don

Me not no Oxford don
me a simple immigrant
from Clapham Common
I didn't graduate
I immigrate

But listen Mr Oxford don
I'm a man on de run
and a man on de run
is a dangerous one

I ent have no gun
I ent have no knife
but mugging de Queen's English
is the story of my life

I dont need no axe
to split/ up yu syntax
I dont need no hammer
to mash/ up yu grammar

I warning you Mr Oxford don
I'm a wanted man
and a wanted man
is a dangerous one

Dem accuse me of assault
on de Oxford dictionary/
imagine a concise peaceful man like me/
dem want me serve time
for inciting rhyme to riot
but I tekking it quiet
down here in Clapham Common

I'm not a violent man Mr Oxford don
I only armed wit mih human breath
but human breath
is a dangerous weapon

So mek dem send one big word after me
I ent serving no jail sentence
I slashing suffix in self-defence
I bashing future wit present tense
and if necessary

I making de Queen's English accessory/to my offence

JOHN AGARD

Poetry for Supper

'Listen, now, verse should be as natural
As the small tuber that feeds on muck
And grows slowly from obtuse soil
To the white flower of immortal beauty.'

'Natural, hell! What was it Chaucer
Said once about the long toil
That goes like blood to the poem's making?
Leave it to nature and the verse sprawls,
Limp as bindweed, if it break at all
Life's iron crust. Man, you must sweat
And rhyme your guts taut, if you'd build
Your verse a ladder.'
                        'You speak as though
No sunlight ever surprised your mind
Groping on its cloudy path.'

'Sunlight's a thing that needs a window
Before it enter a dark room.
Windows don't happen.'
                        So two old poets,
Hunched at their beer in the low haze
Of an inn parlour, while the talk ran
Noisily by them, glib with prose.

R. S. THOMAS

On Being Chosen for A Schools Anthology

Mostly shame, I suppose, at inadequacies
explained away: the right rhyme chosen
for the wrong reason. And tiptoed voices
nibbling at a line which once was fact.

My own two kids could tell them: the slapped
face and the breakfast roar of the bore who sat
cuddling himself in the flat's best corner.

If the truth were known, it is nothing I have
written should be shown in a cloth book in a
cold classroom. But myself in a desk I have
not outgrown with the innocents ringed
around me—pausing as I put in my thumb,
exclaiming as I draw a plum, applauding as I make
the private joke I have in time become.

EDWIN BROCK

The Secret

Two girls discover
the secret of life
in a sudden line of
        poetry.

I who don't know the
secret wrote
the line. They
        told me

(through a third person)
they had found it
but not what it was
        not even

what line it was. No doubt
by now, more than a week
later, they have forgotten
        the secret,

the line, the name of
the poem. I love them
for finding what
        I can't find,

and for loving me
for the line I wrote,
and for forgetting it
        so that

a thousand times, till death
finds them, they may
discover it again, in other
        lines

in other
happenings. And for
wanting to know it,
        for

assuming there is
such a secret, yes,
for that
        most of all.

DENISE LEVERTOV

Word

The word bites like a fish
Shall I throw it back free
Arrowing to that sea
Where thoughts lash tail and fin?
Or shall I pull it in
To rhyme upon a dish?

STEPHEN SPENDER

The Poem

It is only a little twig
With a green bud at the end;
But if you plant it,
And water it,
And set it where the sun will be above it,
It will grow into a tall bush
With many flowers,
And leaves which thrust hither and thither
Sparkling.
From its roots will come freshness,
And beneath it the grass-blades
Will bend and recover themselves,
And clash one upon another
In the blowing wind.

But if you take my twig
And throw it into a closet
With mousetraps and blunted tools,
It will shrivel and waste.
And, some day,
When you open the door,
You will think it an old twisted nail,
And sweep it into the dust bin
With other rubbish.

AMY LOWELL

Alphabeast

Five, I must have been, trailing him
At school through a thicket of print
Down that long afternoon.
No sign in thorned confusion. I raised
My head, Miss said: "You're not trying," I returned
To the grey pages—without warning
He roared out at me, a revealed beast
From a trick picture (can you find our friend
Amid the jungle?) I'd both hands full
With clinging to his tail.

We cleared, in one elated leap,
Tracts of desolation—graded
Readers flickered past us
Like coloured milestones—were gone. I glimpsed
Idiotic toytowns, knocked shocked, skittle-stiff
Policemen toppling; then we were on
To bigger worlds, where moon and sun
Came closer, and his purring filled my ears
Always. My skull vaulted island seas.
His tongue was my pillow.

Worlds within words. I grew and learned
To come, as I grew, at his call.
I came ashamed that no
Photo conjured partner, taste or place
Like his print on well-thumbed white. He became quite
The ogre, cheapening other worlds
Unfairly with his, I couldn't speak
To outsiders; woke up locked in a tall
Glass-walled tower. Although I chattered,
It was only from cold.

How do you unlearn words, return
Them to innocent shapes? I tried
Staring him dumb, and saw
More and more, his features mirrored back
At mine from the glass, saw then it would take death
Or madness to split us; paced the length
Of my cage, coming to terms with new
Strength and old weaknesses, ventured a look
At worlds beyond walls, decided *yes*
And sprang towards the glass.

COLIN ROWBOTHAM

Butterfly

once
in a sudden act
of artless clumsiness
I caught and caged
a butterfly
within a net of words

stunned
it fell
and stuttered across the page
leaving a trail
of watery blood
behind it

I massaged it with metaphors
injected it with images
and finally staged
a simile resuscitation
but in vain:

those light bright flutterings
of pale lemon loveliness
flickered and faintly faded
into stillness

sadly
I pinned it
lifeless and unlovely
to the page
and catalogued it carefully away
with the rest of my
dusty
collection

SUE KELLY

from **Talking With The Taxman About Poetry**

Sung by Billy Bragg on the album of the same name (Go Discs)

Sorry to bother you.
>>> Citizen taxman!
No thanks . . .
>>> Don't worry . . .
>>>>>> I'd rather stand.
I've come to see you
>>> on a delicate matter:
the place
>>> of the poet
>>>>>> in a workers' land.
Along with
>>> storekeepers
>>>>>> and land users
I'm taxable too,
>>> and am bound by the law.
Your demand
>>> for the half-year
>>>>>> is 500 roubles,
and for not filling forms in—25 more.
My labour's
>>> no different
>>>>>> from any other labour.
Examine these figures
>>> of loss and gain,
the production
>>> costs
>>>>>> I have been facing,
the raw material
>>> I had to obtain.
With the notion of "rhyme"
>>> you're acquainted,
>>>>>> of course?
When a line of ours
>>> ends with a word
>>>>>> like "plum"
in the next line but one
>>> we repeat
>>>>>> the syllable

with some other word
            that goes
                  "tiddle-ti-tum".
A rhyme
      is an IOU,
           as you'd put it.
"Pay two lines later"
          is the regulation.
So you seek
          the small change of inflexion, suffix
in the depleted till
         of declensions,
             conjugations.
You shove
      a word
        into a line of poetry
but it just won't go—
         you push and it snaps.
Upon my honour,
        Citizen taxman,
words
    cost poets a pretty penny in cash.
As we poets see it,
        a barrel
          the rhyme is,
a barrel of dynamite,
        the fuse is
          each line.
The line starts smoking,
        exploding the line is,
and the stanza
      blows
     a city
       sky-high.
Where to find rhymes,
        in what tariff list,
that hit the bull's eye
       with never a failure?

Maybe
      a handful of them
            still exist
faraway somewhere
           in Venezuela.
I have to scour
        freezing
           and tropical climes.
I flounder in debt,
         I get advance payments.
My travel expenses
        bear in mind.
Poetry—
      all poetry—
           is an exploration.
Poetry
     is just like mining radium.
To gain just a gram
          you must labour a year.
Tons of lexicon ore
        excavating
all for the sake of one precious word,
But
   how searing
        the heat of this word is
alongside
     the smouldering
        heap of waste.
There are the words
        that go rousing, stirring
millions of hearts
      from age to age.

VLADIMIR MAYAKOVSKY
(trans. Peter Tempest)

What the Chairman Told Tom

POETRY? It's a hobby.
I run model trains.
Mr Shaw there breeds pigeons.

It's not work. You don't sweat.
Nobody pays for it.
You *could* advertise soap.

Art, that's opera; or repertory—
The Desert Song.
Nancy was in the chorus.

But to ask for twelve pounds a week—
married, aren't you?—
you've got a nerve.

How could I look a bus conductor
in the face
if I paid you twelve pounds?

Who says it's poetry, anyhow?
My ten year old
can do it *and* rhyme.

I get three thousand and expenses
a car, vouchers,
but I'm an accountant.

They do what I tell them,
my company.
What do *you* do?

Nasty little words, nasty long words,
it's unhealthy.
I want to wash when I meet a poet.

They're Reds, addicts,
all delinquents.
What they write is rot.

Mr Hines says so, and he's a schoolteacher,
he ought to know.
Go and find *work*.

BASIL BUNTING

★ **Performances.** In different ways, the poems in this section all show us poets writing about writing. Read the poems through and then, in small groups, make the following radio programme.

BBC Radio 4: Poetry Please
Your producer has asked you to work in teams of four or five to make a five-minute programme on the theme 'poets on poetry'. Select, say, four poems from here or elsewhere, share out the readings using different voices, decide on the best order, script your introduction and linking passages, and record your programme on a cassette tape.

★ **Framing your picture.** Fleur Adcock's poem *Leaving the Tate* (p. 68) shifts between two sets of images—'the indoor pictures' in the Tate Gallery she has just visited and 'the outdoor pictures' that she suddenly becomes aware of when she looks at the world outside the gallery.

Read the poem through carefully. Notice how she looks at things with fresh eyes, framing various details as if looking through the viewfinder of a camera.

The poem lends itself to illustration. Think about her mind as a camera. How might you relate the picture-gallery images she's just seen to the new, outdoor 'pictures'? 'You're in charge of the hanging committee.' Illustrate the poem.

★ **Metaphors.** In this section the poet is . . . an acrobat (p. 70) . . . a 'man on de run' (p. 72) . . . a gardener (p. 76) . . . a butterfly collector (p. 78) . . . one of the workers (p. 79) . . . But, are poets workers? Have a look at *What the Chairman Told Tom* (p. 82), according to Basil Bunting, over twenty years ago. Is the chairman right?

People

Born Yesterday

for Sally Amis

Tightly-folded bud,
I have wished you something
None of the others would:
Not the usual stuff
About being beautiful,
Or running off a spring
Of innocence and love—
They will all wish you that,
And should it prove possible,
Well, you're a lucky girl.

But if it shouldn't, then
May you be ordinary;
Have, like other women,
An average of talents:
Not ugly, not good-looking,
Nothing uncustomary
To pull you off your balance,
That, unworkable itself,
Stops all the rest from working.
In fact, may you be dull—
If that is what a skilled,
Vigilant, flexible,
Unemphasised, enthralled
Catching of happiness is called.

PHILIP LARKIN

Follower

My father worked with a horse-plough,
His shoulders globed like a full sail strung
Between the shafts and the furrow.
The horses strained at his clicking tongue.

An expert. He would set the wing
And fit the bright steel-pointed sock.
The sod rolled over without breaking.
At the headrig, with a single pluck

Of reins, the sweating team turned round
And back into the land. His eye
Narrowed and angled at the ground,
Mapping the furrow exactly.

I stumbled in his hob-nailed wake,
Fell sometimes on the polished sod;
Sometimes he rode me on his back
Dipping and rising to his plod.

I wanted to grow up and plough,
To close one eye, stiffen my arm.
All I ever did was follow
In his broad shadow round the farm.

I was a nuisance, tripping, falling,
Yapping always. But today
It is my father who keeps stumbling
Behind me, and will not go away.

SEAMUS HEANEY

To Our Daughter

And she is beautiful, our daughter.
Only six months, but a person.
She turns to look at everything, out walking.
All so precious. I mustn't disturb it with words.
People are like great clowns,
Blossom like balloons, black pigeons like eagles,
Water beyond belief.

She holds out her hand to air,
Sea, sky, wind, sun, movement, stillness,
And wants to hold them all.
My finger is her earth connection, me, and earth.

Her head is like an apple, or an egg.
Skin stretched fine over a strong casing,
Her whole being developing from within
And from without: the answer.

And she sings, long notes from the belly or the throat,
Her legs kick her feet up to her nose,
She rests—laid still like a large rose.
She is our child,
The world is not hers, she has to win it.

JENNIFER ARMITAGE

Balloons

Since Christmas they have lived with us,
Guileless and clear,
Oval soul-animals,
Taking up half the space,
Moving and rubbing on the silk

Invisible air drifts,
Giving a shriek and pop
When attacked, then scooting to rest, barely trembling.
Yellow cathead, blue fish—
Such queer moons we live with

Instead of dead furniture!
Straw mats, white walls
And these travelling
Globes of thin air, red, green,
Delighting

The heart like wishes or free
Peacocks blessing
Old ground with a feather
Beaten in starry metals.
Your small

Brother is making
His balloon squeak like a cat.
Seeming to see
A funny pink world he might eat on the other side of it,
He bites,

Then sits
Back, fat jug
Contemplating a world clear as water,
A red
Shred in his little fist.

SYLVIA PLATH

The Fat Black Woman Goes Shopping

Shopping in London winter
is a real drag for the fat black woman
going from store to store
in search of accommodating clothes
and de weather so cold

Look at the frozen thin mannequins
fixing her with grin
and de pretty face salesgals
exchanging slimming glances
thinking she don't notice

Lord is aggravating

Nothing soft and bright and billowing
to flow like breezy sunlight
when she walking

The fat black woman curses in Swahili/Yoruba
and nation language under her breathing
all this journeying and journeying

The fat black woman could only conclude
that when it come to fashion
the choice is lean

Nothing much beyond size 14

GRACE NICHOLS

A Civil Servant

While in this cavernous place employed
  Not once was I aware
Of my officious other-self
  Poised high above me there,

My self reversed, my rage-less part,
  A slimy yellow-ish cone—
Drip, drip; drip, drip—so down the years
  I stalagmatised in stone.

Now pilgrims to the cave, who come
  To chip off what they can,
Prod me with child-like merriment:
  'Look, look! It's like a man!'

ROBERT GRAVES

Death in Leamington

She died in the upstairs bedroom
  By the light of the ev'ning star
That shone through the plate glass window
  From over Leamington Spa.

Beside her the lonely crochet
  Lay patiently and unstirred,
But the fingers that would have work'd it
  Were dead as the spoken word.

And Nurse came in with the tea-things
  Breast high 'mid the stands and chairs—
But Nurse was alone with her own little soul,
  And the things were alone with theirs.

She bolted the big round window,
  She let the blinds unroll,
She set a match to the mantle,
  She covered the fire with coal.

And 'Tea!' she said in a tiny voice
  'Wake up! It's nearly five.'
  Oh! Chintzy, chintzy cheeriness,
  Half dead and half alive!

Do you know that the stucco is peeling?
  Do you know that the heart will stop?
From those yellow Italianate arches
  Do you hear the plaster drop?

Nurse looked at the silent bedstead,
  At the gray, decaying face,
As the calm of a Leamington ev'ning
  Drifted into the place.

She moved the table of bottles
  Away from the bed to the wall;
And tiptoeing gently over the stairs
  Turned down the gas in the hall.

JOHN BETJEMAN

Mrs Root

Busybody, nosey-parker
lacking the vast discretion of most
was this woman. The self-cast
chief mourner at funerals, worker
at weddings, she could sniff out death
in a doctor's optimism, joggle
a maiden's mind (button-holed on the front path)
till virginity bit like filed teeth.

Prepared, without discrimination,
friend and enemy for the grave.
Washed, talcumed them all. A woman
who wore such ceremonies like a glove,
could console a grief-struck household
that hardly knew her name, and then
collect money for a wreath fit to wield
at a Queen's passing. Death-skilled
but no less wedding-wise,
her hand stitched the perfecting dart
in bridal satin; she brought report
of cars arriving, clear skies
towards the church. They were her tears
(pew-stifled) from which the happiest
laughter billowed confetti outside the black doors.
Of best wishes, loudest were hers.

And nobody thanked her. Why doesn't
she mind her own business? they said
who'd leant upon her. Crude and peasant-like
her interest in brides, and the dead.
I thought so too, yet still was loth
to add my voice, sensing that
my secret poems were like her actions: both
pried into love and savoured death.

TONY CONNOR

91

The High Tree

There was a tree higher than clouds or lightning,
higher than any plane could fly.

England huddled under its roots; leaves from it
fluttered on Europe out of the sky.

The weather missed it: it was higher than weather,
up in the sunshine, always dry.

It was a refuge. When you sat in its branches
threatening strangers passed you by.

Nothing could find you. Even friendly people,
if you invited them to try,

couldn't climb very far. It made them dizzy:
they'd shiver and shut their eyes and cry,

and you'd have to guide them down again, backwards,
wishing they hadn't climbed so high.

So it wasn't a social tree. It was perfect
for someone solitary and shy

who liked gazing out over miles of history,
watching it happen, like a spy,

and was casual about heights, but didn't fancy
coming down again to defy

the powers below. Odd that they didn't notice
all this climbing on the sly,

and odder still, if they knew, that they didn't ban it.
Knowing them now, you'd wonder why.

FLEUR ADCOCK

The Railway Children

When we climbed the slopes of the cutting
We were eye-level with the white cups
Of the telegraph poles and the sizzling wires.

Like lovely freehand they curved for miles
East and miles west beyond us, sagging
Under their burden of swallows.

We were small and thought we knew nothing
Worth knowing. We thought words travelled the wires
In the shiny pouches of raindrops,

Each one seeded full with the light
Of the sky, the gleam of the lines, and ourselves
So infinitesimally scaled

We could stream through the eye of a needle.

SEAMUS HEANEY

Blackness

Blackness is me,
For I am black.
What mundane pow'r can change that fact?
If I should roam the world afar;
If I should soar the heights of stars;
If earthly honours I attract,
I'd still be black—
For black is black
And there is naught can change that fact.
Africa's my mother's name;
And it is she from whence I came.
That's why I'm black,
For so is she.
Blackness is our identity.
Blackness is what we want to be.
You are white;
Whiteness is you.
My Africa is not your mother,
But yet you are—you are my brother!

GLYNE WALROND

Docker

There, in the corner, staring at his drink.
The cap juts like a gantry's crossbeam,
Cowling plated forehead and sledgehead jaw.
Speech is clamped in the lips' vice.

That fist would drop a hammer on a Catholic—
Oh yes, that kind of thing could start again;
The only Roman collar he tolerates
Smiles all round his sleek pint of porter.

Mosaic imperatives bang home like rivets;
God is a foreman with certain definite views
Who orders life in shifts of work and leisure.
A factory horn will blare the Resurrection.

He sits, strong and blunt as a Celtic cross,
Clearly used to silence and an armchair:
Tonight the wife and children will be quiet
At slammed door and smoker's cough in the hall.

SEAMUS HEANEY

Unrecorded Speech

She says 'How was you?' Kissing. 'Come on in,
I'm all of a muck-sweat, having a merry-go-round;
you've caught me doing my work.'
She doesn't clean, but circumvents the dirt.
Chairs stand on tables—'All of a tizz-wozz.'
(Has that been spelt before?) 'A lick of paint,'
she says, propping her brush in turps,
'freshens things up a bit.' She paints the door
and skirting-boards; washes white window-veils.
Houses, bedsitters, flats, extend herself.
She makes the best of it, but likes a move;
it's like a change of dress, changing address.
I've lost count of the changes. 'Home at last!'
is said too often to be credible.
We'll write it on her tomb, or jar of ash,
unless she sees us out.
She says 'The poor old lady,' of someone
no older than herself.
'She's gone a bit—you know dear—gone a bit
doo-lally. Poor old thing. It takes all sorts—'
From childhood she remembers sparkling frost,
and walking out in it in Christmas clothes—
a coat her mother made her—vivid mauve—
'so bright against the snow.'
'And of a Friday afternoon
the teacher read to us. That was the best.'
Stories have been essential food since then.
Peg's Paper, H.E. Bates, Hardy and all
except romances; 'that don't interest me.'
She fills her days 'somehow', since Hubby died,
but she has grown since then.
'All in a lifetime dear,' she says of death.
Her words may be dead language soon;
that's why I write them down. They will be heard
'never no more', as she said at the birth
of my husband, her only child,
proving that double negatives mean 'No'.

ANNA ADAMS

Post Office

The queue's right out through the glass doors
to the street: Thursday, pension day.
They built this Post Office too small.
Of course, the previous one was smaller—
a tiny prefab, next to the betting-shop,
says the man who's just arrived;
and the present one, at which we're queuing,
was cherry-trees in front of a church.
The church was where the supermarket is:
'My wife and I got married in that church'
the man says. 'We hold hands sometimes
when we're standing waiting at the checkout—
have a little moment together!' He laughs.
The queue shuffles forward a step.
Three members of it silently vow
never to grow old in this suburb;
one vows never to grow old at all.
'I first met her over there' the man says,
'on that corner where the bank is now.
The other corner was Williams Brothers—
remember Williams Brothers? They gave you tokens,
tin money, like, for your dividend.'
The woman in front of him remembers.
She nods, and swivels her loose lower denture,
remembering Williams Brothers' metal tokens,
and the marble slab on the cheese-counter,
and the carved mahogany booth where you went to pay.
The boy in front of her is chewing gum;
his jaws rotate with the same motion
as hers: to and fro, to and fro.

FLEUR ADCOCK

London–Tokyo

There is no other creature like
The one fate sets beside us in a 'plane:
The vivacious grandmother, experienced traveller;
The amateur technician—'Don't look now, but
That number four propeller seems to be fluctuating madly—';
The convent schoolgirl mooning over Simone Weil;
The Indian mystic with his blissful flies undone;
The British maniac scribbling postcards all the night,
Counting and re-counting his collected works
That he stacks and shuffles, deals like decks of cards.

However wild a silence we may keep,
We moodily involve them in our private glooms:
We turn their glance upon the old moon lying on its back,
And wolf their breakfasts on our individual trays.
He knows 'the little boys' room' at every gritty port,
While she, 'at crazy prices', snaps up fags and lipsticks, drink
    and scent.

Reaching their several destinations, they
Matily wish us 'Happy Landings!' while we try
To smile blandly as the shuddering jet-plane takes
Its running jump at yet another sky.

JAMES KIRKUP

After the Fireworks

Back into the light and warmth,
Boots clogged with mud, toes
Welded to wedges of cold flesh,
The children warm their hands on mugs
While, on remembered lawns, the flash
Of fireworks dazzles night;
Sparklers spray and rockets swish,
Soar high and break in falling showers
Of glitter; the bonfire gallivants,
Its lavish flames shimmy, prance,
And lick the straddling guy.
We wait for those great leaves of heat
And broken necklaces of light
To dim and die.
And then the children go to bed.
Tomorrow they will search the grey ground
For debris of tonight: the sad
And saturated cardboard stems,
The fallen rocket sticks, the charred
Hubs of catherine-wheels;
Then, having gathered all they've found,
They'll leave them scattered carelessly
For us to clear away.
But now the children are asleep,
And you and I sit silently
And hear, from far off in the night,
The last brave rocket burst and fade.
We taste the darkness in the light,
Reflect that fireworks are not cheap
And ask ourselves uneasily
If, even now, we've fully paid.

VERNON SCANNELL

Ful semely after hir mete she raught[3].
And sikerly she was of greet desport[4],
And ful plesaunt, and amyable of port,
And peyned hire to countrefete cheere
Of court, and to been estatlich of manere[5],
And to ben holden digne of reverence[6].
But, for to speken of hire conscience,
She was so charitable and so pitous
She wolde wepe, if that she saugh a mous
Kaught in a trappe, if it were deed or bledde.
Of smale houndes hadde she that she fedde
With rosted flessh, or milk and wastelbreed[7].
But soore wepte she if oon of hem were deed,
Or if men smoot it with a yerde smerte;
And al was conscience and tendre herte.
Ful semyly hir wympul[8] pynched[9] was,
Hir nose tretys[10], hir eyen greye as glas,
Hir mouth ful smal, and thereto softe and reed;
But sikerly she hadde a fair forheed;
It was almoost a spanne brood[11], I trowe;
For, hardily, she was nat undergrowe.
Ful fetys was hir cloke, as I was war.
Of small coral aboute hire arm she bar
A peire of bedes, gauded al with grene,
And theron heng a brooch of gold ful sheene,
On which ther was first write a crowned A,
And after *Amor vincit omnia*[12].

[3] reached
[4] and certainly she was a very cheerful person
[5] she took pains to imitate courtly behaviour, and to be dignified in her bearing
[6] held worthy
[7] fine wheat bread
[8] wimple
[9] pleated
[10] well shaped
[11] a span broad
[12] Love conquers all

(from the *General Prologue* to
The Canterbury Tales)
GEOFFREY CHAUCER

Ten Types of Hospital Visitor

I

The first enters wearing the neon armour
Of virtue.
Ceaselessly firing all-purpose smiles
At everyone present
She destroys hope
In the breasts of the sick,
Who realize instantly
That they are incapable of surmounting
Her ferocious goodwill.

Such courage she displays
In the face of human disaster!

Fortunately, she does not stay long.
After a speedy trip round the ward
In the manner of a nineteen-thirties destroyer
Showing the flag in the Mediterranean,
She returns home for a week
—With luck, longer—
Scorched by the heat of her own worthiness.

II

The second appears, a melancholy splurge
Of theological colours;
Taps heavily about like a healthy vulture
Distributing deep-frozen hope.

The patients gaze at him cautiously.
Most of them, as yet uncertain of the realities
Of heaven, hell-fire, or eternal emptiness,
Play for safety
By accepting his attentions
With just-concealed apathy,
Except one old man, who cries
With newly sharpened hatred,
'Shove off! Shove off!
'Shove . . . shove . . . shove . . . shove
Off!
Just you
Shove!'

III

The third skilfully deflates his weakly smiling victim
By telling him
How the lobelias are doing,
How many kittens the cat had,
How the slate came off the scullery roof,
And how no one has visited the patient for a fortnight
Because everybody
Had colds and feared to bring the jumpy germ
Into hospital.

The patient's eyes
Ice over. He is uninterested
In lobelias, the cat, the slate, the germ.
Flat on his back, drip-fed, his face
The shade of a newly dug-up Pharaoh,
Wearing his skeleton outside his skin,
Yet his wits as bright as a lighted candle,
He is concerned only with the here, the now,

And requires to speak
Of nothing but his present predicament.

It is not permitted.

IV

The fourth attempts to cheer
His aged mother with light jokes
Menacing as shell-splinters.
'They'll soon have you jumping round
Like a gazelle,' he says.
'Playing in the football team.'
Quite undeterred by the sight of kilos
Of plaster, chains, lifting-gear,
A pair of lethally designed crutches,
'You'll be leap-frogging soon,' he says.
'Swimming ten lengths of the baths.'

At these unlikely prophecies
The old lady stares fearfully
At her sick, sick offspring
Thinking he has lost his reason—

Which, alas, seems to be the case.

V

The fifth, a giant from the fields
With suit smelling of milk and hay,
Shifts uneasily from one bullock foot
To the other, as though to avoid
Settling permanently in the antiseptic landscape.
Occasionally he looses a scared glance
Sideways, as though fearful of what intimacy
He may blunder on, or that the walls
Might suddenly close in on him.

He carries flowers, held lightly in fingers
The size and shape of plantains,
Tenderly kisses his wife's cheek

—The brush of a child's lips—
Then balances, motionless, for thirty minutes
On the thin chair.

At the end of visiting time
He emerges breathless,
Blinking with relief, into the safe light.

He does not appear to notice
The dusk.

VI

The sixth visitor says little,
Breathes reassurance,
Smiles securely.
Carries no black passport of grapes
And visa of chocolate. Has a clutch
Of clean washing.

Unobtrusively stows it
In the locker; searches out more.
Talks quietly to the Sister
Out of sight, out of earshot, of the patient.
Arrives punctually as a tide.
Does not stay the whole hour.

Even when she has gone
The patient seems to sense her there:
An upholding
Presence.

VII

The seventh visitor
Smells of bar-room after-shave.
Often finds his friend
Sound asleep: whether real or feigned
Is never determined.

He does not mind; prowls the ward
In search of second-class, lost-face patients
With no visitors
And who are pretending to doze
Or read paperbacks.

He probes relentlessly the nature
Of each complaint, and is swift with such
Dilutions of confidence as,
'Ah! You'll be worse
Before you're better.'

Five minutes before the bell punctuates
Visiting time, his friend opens an alarm-clock eye.
The visitor checks his watch.
Market day. The Duck and Pheasant will be still open.

Courage must be refuelled.

VIII

The eighth visitor looks infinitely
More decayed, ill and infirm than any patient.
His face is an expensive grey.

He peers about with antediluvian eyes
As though from the other end
Of time.
He appears to have risen from the grave
To make this appearance.
There is a whiff of white flowers about him;
The crumpled look of a slightly used shroud.
Slowly he passes the patient
A bag of bullet-proof
Home-made biscuits,
A strong, death-dealing cake—
'To have with your tea,'
Or a bowl of fruit so weighty
It threatens to break
His glass fingers.

The patient, encouraged beyond measure,
Thanks him with enthusiasm, not for
The oranges, the biscuits, the cake,
But for the healing sight
Of someone patently worse
Than himself. He rounds the crisis-corner;
Begins a recovery.

IX

The ninth visitor is life.

X

The tenth visitor
Is not usually named.

CHARLES CAUSLEY

John Henry

John Henry was 'a steel driving man'—a railroad worker whose task was to drill holes in the rocks for the dynamite charges by striking the drill with a hammer. The legend tells of a contest between John Henry and a steam drill during the construction of the C. & O. tunnel at Big Bend, West Virginia. There are many versions of the John Henry story and the sequence of the verses is frequently uncertain.

When John Henry was a little boy,
Sitting upon his father's knee,
His father said, 'Look here, my boy,
You must be a steel driving man like me,
You must be a steel driving man like me.'

John Henry had a little wife,
And the dress she wore was red;
The last thing before he died,
He said, 'Be true to me when I'm dead,
Oh, be true to me when I'm dead.'

John Henry's wife asked him for fifteen cents,
And he said he didn't have but a dime,
Said, 'If you wait till the rising sun goes down,
I'll borrow it from the man in the mine,
I'll borrow it from the man in the mine.'

John Henry went upon the mountain,
Just to drive himself some steel.
The rocks were so tall and John Henry so small,
He said lay down hammer and squeal,
He said lay down hammer and squeal.

John Henry started on the right-hand side,
And the steam drill started on the left.
He said, 'Before I'd let that steam drill beat me down,
I'd hammer my fool self to death,
Oh, I'd hammer my fool self to death.'

The steam drill started at half past six,
John Henry started the same time.
John Henry struck bottom at half past eight,
And the steam drill didn't bottom till nine,
And the steam drill didn't bottom till nine.

John Henry said to his captain,
'A man, he ain't nothing but a man,
Before I'd let that steam drill beat me down,
I'd die with the hammer in my hand,
Oh, I'd die with the hammer in my hand.'

John Henry said to his shaker,
'Shaker, why don't you sing just a few more rounds?
And before the setting sun goes down,
You're gonna hear this hammer of mine sound,
You're gonna hear this hammer of mine sound.'

John Henry hammered on the mountain,
He hammered till half past three,
He said, 'This big Bend Tunnel on the C. & O. road
Is going to be the death of me,
Lord! is going to be the death of me.'

John Henry had a little baby boy,
You could hold him in the palm of your hand.
The last words before he died,
'Son, you must be a steel driving man,
Son, you must be a steel driving man.'

John Henry had a little woman,
And the dress she wore was red,
She went down the railroad track and never come back,
Said she was going where John Henry fell dead,
Said she was going where John Henry fell dead.

John Henry hammering on the mountain,
As the whistle blew for half past two,
The last word I heard him say,
'Captain, I've hammered my insides in two,
Lord, I've hammered my insides in two.'

collected GUY B. JOHNSON

Rugby League Game

Sport is absurd, and sad.
Those grown men, just look,
In those dreary long blue shorts,
Those ringed stockings, Edwardian,
Balding pates, and huge
Fat knees that ought to be heroes'.

Grappling, hooking, gallantly tackling—
Is all this courage really necessary?—
Taking their good clean fun
So solemnly, they run each other down
With earnest keenness, for the honour of
Virility, the cap, the county side.

Like great boys they roll each other
In the mud of public Saturdays,
Groping their blind way back
To noble youth, away from the bank,
The wife, the pram, the spin drier,
Back to the spartan freedom of the field.

Back, back to the days when boys
Were men, still hopeful, and untamed.
That was then: a gay
And golden age ago.
Now, in vain, domesticated,
Men try to be boys again.

JAMES KIRKUP

The Telephone Call

They asked me 'Are you sitting down?
Right? This is Universal Lotteries',
they said. 'You've won the top prize,
the Ultra-super Global Special.
What would you do with a million pounds?
Or, actually, with more than a million—
not that it makes a lot of difference
once you're a millionaire.' And they laughed.

'Are you OK?' they asked—'Still there?
Come on, now, tell us, how does it feel?'
I said 'I just . . . I can't believe it!'
They said 'That's what they all say.
What else? Go on, tell us about it.'
I said 'I feel the top of my head
has floated off, out through the window,
revolving like a flying saucer.'

'That's unusual' they said. 'Go on.'
I said 'I'm finding it hard to talk.
My throat's gone dry, my nose is tingling.
I think I'm going to sneeze—or cry.'
'That's right' they said, 'don't be ashamed
of giving way to your emotions.
It isn't every day you hear
you're going to get a million pounds.

Relax, now, have a little cry;
we'll give you a moment . . .' 'Hang on!' I said.
'I haven't bought a lottery ticket
for years and years. And what did you say
the company's called?' They laughed again.
'Not to worry about a ticket.
We're Universal. We operate
a Retrospective Chances Module.

Nearly everyone's bought a ticket
in some lottery or another,
once at least. We buy up the files,
feed the names into our computer,
and see who the lucky person is.'
'Well, that's incredible' I said.
'It's marvellous. I still can't quite . . .
I'll believe it when I see the cheque.'

'Oh,' they said, 'there's no cheque.'
'But the money?' 'We don't deal in money.
Experiences are what we deal in.
You've had a great experience, right?
Exciting? Something you'll remember?
That's your prize. So congratulations
from all of us at Universal.
Have a nice day!' And the line went dead.

FLEUR ADCOCK

★ **Dialogues.** There are various ways to build a piece of writing out of things that you have heard people say. Below we suggest two but, first, look at the poem *Unrecorded Speech* (p. 96). Hear it read aloud, one person taking the dialogue, the other the rest. What impression do you get of the writer's mother-in-law?

Make up a similar sort of portrait in one of these ways:

(i) *In pairs*, list the phrases and sayings that your family and friends use regularly. Against each one make a note of when these phrases are used. For example, you might have: 'We didn't do that when I was at school'—Dad or Mum about talking in class. 'They're ace/great/the greatest . . .'—friends about a favourite group. When you have a list of ten or twelve sayings, select the ones that go together and make up a portrait of a single person or group of people out of the things they say or that are said about them.

(ii) *On your own*, think back over the past few days and try to recall any snatches of conversation that you have overheard —maybe between people sitting near you on the bus, or passing you in the street; they may be whispered comments, ordinary chat, or shouted remarks. Even if it's only one exchange that you cannot recall exactly, it doesn't matter. Whatever you remember, write it down, setting it out as a play, i.e. with the person's name in the left margin and their remarks alongside, starting a new line for each speech.

Compare your notes with those of your partner and decide which situation you can develop most easily into a short scene. Invent the conversation that might take place, writing out your script and acting directions as you go. Rehearse and act out your dialogues, either as live or taped performances.

★ **Portraits.** There are several 'pen-portraits' in this section—a docker (p. 95), a civil servant (p. 89), a black woman going shopping (p. 88) and a whole series of typical hospital visitors (pp. 103–108).

In pairs or small groups, read through these poems aloud, sharing out the lines where you can.

As you hear each poem, jot down *individually* no more than one or two lines or phrases from the poem that seem to you to capture the character of the person described.

When you have heard all the poems, go back and compare your 'key phrases' with those of the others and decide what you think is the main idea of each 'pen-portrait'.

★ **Performances.** There are several varieties of spoken English to try out when you read the following poems:

—*John Henry* (pp. 109–110) is best shared between two voices —one for the narrator, the other for the character's dialogue. Try out your American accents. If you can get someone in the class to provide a guitar 'backing', so much the better.

—*The Monk* (p. 100) and *The Prioresse* (p. 101) were written in Middle English six centuries ago. These are ones for individuals to rehearse and read aloud for the rest of the class. Don't be frightened of making the wrong sounds. As a rough guide, 'a' sounds are often flat—'was', 'whan'; and the final 'e' is often pronounced—'hadde', 'heere'. Have a go! If you want to hear how Chaucer's English sounds, listen to the cassette, *Prologue to the Canterbury Tales*, Argo.

—*The Fat Black Woman Goes Shopping* (p. 88) and *Blackness* (p. 94) are by West Indian writers. Again, they are best spoken by single voices. See if you can catch the Caribbean sound as you read the poems aloud.

Religious Experience

Vertue

Sweet day, so cool, so calm, so bright,
The bridall of the earth and skie:
The dew shall weep thy fall to night;
    For thou must die.

Sweet rose, whose hue angrie and brave
Bids the rash gazer wipe his eye:
Thy root is ever in its grave,
    And thou must die.

Sweet spring, full of sweet dayes and roses,
A box where sweets[1] compacted lie;   [1]perfumes
My musick shows ye have your closes,
    And all must die.

Onely a sweet and vertuous soul,
Like season'd timber, never gives;
But though the whole world turn to coal,
    Then chiefly lives.

GEORGE HERBERT

Pied Beauty

Glory be to God for dappled things—
    For skies of couple-colour as a brinded cow;
      For rose-moles all in stipple upon trout that swim;
Fresh-firecoal chestnut-falls; finches' wings;
    Landscape plotted and pieced—fold, fallow, and plough;
      And áll trádes, their gear and tackle and trim.
All things counter, original, spare, strange;
    Whatever is fickle, freckled (who knows how?)
      With swift, slow; sweet, sour; adazzle, dim;
He fathers-forth whose beauty is past change:
      Praise him.

GERARD MANLEY HOPKINS

Love

Love bade me welcome: yet my soul drew back,
    Guiltie of dust and sinne.
But quick-ey'd Love, observing me grow slack
    From my first entrance in,
Drew nearer to me, sweetly questioning.
    If I lack'd anything.

A guest, I answer'd, worthy to be here:
    Love said, You shall be he.
I the unkinde, ungratefull? Ah my deare,
    I cannot look on thee.
Love took my hand, and smiling did reply,
    Who made the eyes but I?

Truth Lord, but I have marr'd them: let my shame
    Go where it doth deserve.
And know you not, sayes Love, who bore the blame?
    My deare, then I will serve.
You must sit down, sayes Love, and taste my meat:
    So I did sit and eat.

GEORGE HERBERT

Upon a Dead Man's Head

Your ugly token
My mind hath broken
From worldly lust:
For I have discust
We are but dust,
And die we must.
  It is general
To be mortal:
I have well espied
No man may him hide
From Death hollow-eyed,
With sinews wyderèd[1],
With bones shyderèd,
With his worm-eaten maw,
And his ghastly jaw
Gasping aside,
Naked of hide,
Neither flesh nor fell.
  Then, by my counsel,
Look that ye spell
Well this gospel:
For whereso we dwell
Death will us quell,
And with us mell.
  For all our pampered paunches
There may no fraunchis[2],
Nor worldly bliss,
Redeem us from this:
Our days be dated
To be checkmated
With draughtes of death
Stopping our breath:
Our eyen sinking,
Our bodies stinking,
Our gummes grinning,
Our soules brinning[3].

To whom, then, shall we sue,
For to have rescue,
But to sweet Jesu
On us then for to rue[4]?
  O goodly Child
Of Mary mild,
Then be our shield!
That we be not exiled
To the dyne[5] dale
Of bootless bale[6],
Nor to the lake
Of fiendes black.
  But grant us grace
To see thy Face,
And to purchase
Thine heavenly place,
And thy palace
Full of solace
Above the sky
That is so high;
Eternally
To behold and see
The Trinity!
  Amen.

JOHN SKELTON

---

[1] withered   [2] privilege   [3] burning   [4] be sorry   [5] noisy   [6] torment

119

I Have Not Seen God

I have not seen God face to face
Therefore I cannot fear Him
But I fear lightning and the anger of righteous men,
And this grasping at space
In a night grown huge behind the trembling stars.

I have not seen God face to face
Therefore I cannot worship Him
But I worship mountains that wear a bloom of grapes
In the evening sun; I worship primitive things—
Trees and essential shapes
Of beauty outlined in the world we touch.

I have not see God face to face
Therefore I cannot love Him
But I love the light that quickens wood and stone,
The sudden grace
Lifting a dull pedestrian out of time
And place, to find the Unknown through the known.

PHOEBE HESKETH

Water

If I were called in
To construct a religion
I should make use of water.

Going to church
Would entail a fording
To dry, different clothes;

My litany would employ
Images of sousing,
A furious devout drench,

And I should raise in the east
A glass of water
Where any-angled light
Would congregate endlessly.

PHILIP LARKIN

Be a Butterfly

Don't be a kyatta-pilla
Be a butterfly
old preacher screamed
to illustrate his sermon
of Jesus and the higher life

rivulets of well-earned
sweat sliding down
his muscly mahogany face
in the half-empty school church
we sat shaking with muffling
laughter
watching our mother trying to save
herself from joining the wave

only our father remaining poker face
and afterwards we always went home to
split peas Sunday soup
with dumplings, fufu and pigtail

Don't be a kyatta-pilla
Be a butterfly
Be a butterfly

That was de life preacher
and you was right

GRACE NICHOLS

Not everybody would describe themselves as religious. Why then a section in this collection given over to religious experience? One of the main reasons is that religious feeling has been an inspiration for many writers and has given rise to some of the strongest poetry in the language. Whatever our beliefs may or may not be, a reading of their work provides an insight into their thoughts and feelings and may from time to time provide a flash of recognition. Whether you accept or reject religious belief or are uncertain what you think, reading, talking and writing about it in the light of other people's experience is one of the most useful ways of sorting out your ideas.

★ **Performance.** Gerard Manley Hopkins who wrote the poem *Pied Beauty* on page 117 was a priest. The sheer joyful rush of words as he praises the abundance and variety of the natural world almost bowls us over. In small groups of about five or so, devise a dramatic reading of the poem and when you are pleased with it, perform it for the class or make a tape recording. You could choose to tackle it as a choral piece with all of you speaking together, or you could split the lines between different readers . . . or you could mix both techniques. Whatever you do, try not to lose the life and movement of the verse.

George Herbert who wrote *Vertue* and *Love*, the two poems on pages 116 and 117, was also a parish priest. He wrote in the seventeenth century and the language of the poems may seem a little strange at first. Again, in small groups devise a reading of the poems. The first one, *Vertue*, is probably the easier of the two and could simply be split between four single voices for the main part of each verse with a choral reading of the short last lines. *Love* is a conversation between the writer and Love. It needs some careful thought about who is saying what and can perhaps only be read aloud using two voices.

Going even further back in time we find John Skelton's poem *Upon a Dead Man's Head* (p. 118) which was written in the sixteenth century. It is typical of what one writer described as Skelton's 'headlong voluble, breathless doggerel . . . rattling and clashing on through quick recurring rhymes'. It can be split very effectively between a number of different voices.

Lawrence Ferlinghetti wrote his poem *Christ Climbed Down* (pp. 120–1) in more recent years and questions the modern commercialised Christmas he sees in America. In groups, work out a performance of the poem. There are several American references that you may need to know about: Sears Roebuck is a

124

big mail order firm; Lord Calvert Whiskey is an American brand of alcohol; there is a town called Bethlehem in the American state of Pennsylvania; the Adirondacks is a mountainous region of the States; Humble is an oil company and Saks a very expensive shop; Bing Crosby will continue forever to croon his way through *White* (not Tight) *Christmas*.

The preacher in Grace Nichols' poem on p. 123 exhorts us not to be 'Kyatta-pillas' but to be butterflies. Try to dramatise his message in a small group reading of the poem.

★ **Talking and Writing.** With a partner share your feelings about being in religious places—it may perhaps be a church, cathedral, mosque, synagogue, or temple that you know or have visited. How do you feel when you are there? By yourself, jot down your ideas about the atmosphere and about how you feel; see if you can work them up into a poem that communicates those feelings.

Philip Larkin suggests that if he had to construct a religion he would base it on water. Read his poem *Water* on p. 122 and talk in pairs about why you think he might have thought it a good idea. If *you* were called in to construct a religion what would you choose as the symbol at its centre? Try to set down your ideas in a poem which follows the same pattern as Larkin's poem: you need only substitute your idea for 'water' in the first verse and then develop it from there.

Town and Country

British Weather

It is the merry month of May,
when everything is cold and grey,
the rain is dripping from the trees
and life is like a long disease,

the storm clouds hover round like ghouls,
the birds all sing, because they're fools,
and beds of optimistic flowers
are beaten down by thunder showers,

under a weak and watery sun
nothing seems to be much fun—
exciting as a piece of string,
this is the marvellous British Spring!

GAVIN EWART

IT WAS ONE OF THOSE LONG ENGLISH SUMMER
DAYS THAT SEEM TO GO ON FOR EVER...

Sunken Evening

The green light floods the city square—
　　A sea of fowl and feathered fish,
　　Where squalls of rainbirds dive and splash
And gusty sparrows chop the air.

Submerged, the prawn-blue pigeons feed
　　In sandy grottoes round the Mall,
　　And crusted lobster-buses crawl
Among the fountains' silver weed.

There, like a wreck, with mast and bell,
　　The torn church settles by the bow,
　　While phosphorescent starlings stow
Their mussel shells along the hull.

The oyster-poet, drowned but dry,
　　Rolls a black pearl between his bones;
　　The typist, trapped by telephones,
Gazes in bubbles at the sky.

Till, with the dark, the shallows run,
　　And homeward surges tide and fret—
　　The slow night trawls its heavy net
And hauls the clerk to Surbiton.

LAURIE LEE

Cut Grass

Cut grass lies frail:
Brief is the breath
Mown stalks exhale.
Long, long the death

It dies in the white hours
Of young-leafed June
With chestnut flowers,
With hedges snowlike strewn,

White lilac bowed,
Lost lanes of Queen Anne's lace,
And that high-builded cloud
Moving at summer's pace.

PHILIP LARKIN

October in Clowes Park

The day dispossessed of light. At four o'clock
in the afternoon, a sulphurous, manufactured
twilight, smudging the scummed lake's far side,
leant on the park. Sounds, muffled—
as if the lolling muck clogged them at the source—
crawled to the ear. A skyed ball thudded
to ground, a swan leathered its wings by the island.
I stood and watched a water-hen arrow
shutting silver across the sooty mat
of the lake's surface, an earl's lake,
though these fifty years the corporation's,
and what is left of the extensive estate—
a few acres of scruffy, flat land
framing this wet sore in the minds of property agents—
a public park. All else is built on.
Through swags of trees poked the bare backsides
of encircling villas, garages, gardening sheds,
a ring of lights making the park dimmer.
Boys and men shouldering long rods—
all licensed fishers, by their open way—
scuffled the cinders past me, heading for home,
but I stayed on; the dispossessed day
held me, turned me towards the ruined Hall.
Pulsing in that yellow, luminous, murk
(a trick of the eye), the bits of broken pillar
built into banks, the last upright wall,
the stalactite-hung split shells of stables,
seemed likely to find a voice—such pent-in grief
and anger!—or perhaps to explode silently
with force greater than any known to progress,
wiping the district, town, kingdom, age,
to darkness far deeper than that which fluffed
now at the neat new urinal's outline,
and heaved and beat behind it at the ruins.
Like a thud in the head, suddenly become memory,
stillness was dumb around me. Scrambling up
a heap of refuse, I grabbed at crystalled brick.
Flakes fell from my hand—a gruff tinkle—
no knowledge there of what brought the Hall low,
or concern either. Neither did I care.

Irrecoverably dead, slumped in rank weed
and billowy grass, it mouldered from here to now,
connoting nothing but where my anger stood
and grief enough to pull the sagging smoke down
from the sky, a silent, lethal, swaddling
over the garden I played in as a child,
and over those children—laughter in the branches—
shaking the pear-tree's last sour fruit to ground.

TONY CONNOR

November

The month of the drowned dog. After long rain the land
Was sodden as the bed of an ancient lake,
Treed with iron and birdless. In the sunk lane
The ditch—a seep silent all summer—

Made brown foam with a big voice; that, and my boots
On the lane's scrubbed stones, in the gulleyed leaves,
Against the hill's hanging silence;
Mist silvering the droplets on the bare thorns

Slower than the change of daylight.
In a let of the ditch a tramp was bundled asleep:
Face tucked down into beard, drawn in
Under its hair like a hedgehog's. I took him for dead,

But his stillness separated from the death
Of the rotting grass and the ground. A wind chilled,
And a fresh comfort tightened through him,
Each hand stuffed deeper into the other sleeve.

His ankles, bound with sacking and hairy band,
Rubbed each other, resettling. The wind hardened;
A puff shook a glittering from the thorns,
And again the rain's dragging grey columns

Smudged the farms. In a moment
The fields were jumping and smoking; the thorns
Quivering, riddled with the glassy verticals.
I stayed on under the welding cold

Watching the tramp's face glisten and the drops on his coat
Flash and darken. I thought what strong trust
Slept in him—as the trickling furrows slept,
And the thorn-roots in their grip on darkness;

And the buried stones, taking the weight of winter;
The hill where the hare crouched with clenched teeth.
Rain plastered the land till it was shining
Like hammered lead, and I ran, and in the rushing wood

Shuttered by a black oak leaned.
The keeper's gibbet had owls and hawks
By the neck, weasels, a gang of cats, crows:
Some, stiff, weightless, twirled like dry bark bits

In the drilling rain. Some still had their shape,
Had their pride with it; hung, chins on chests,
Patient to outwait these worst days that beat
Their crowns bare and dripped from their feet.

TED HUGHES

December

The Festive rush. Cold, iron steps vibrate
In memory: that juddering, long ascent
To the top of the playground slide. No losing face
By a climbdown; though I'd shiver, hesitate
On my perch—till, shoved impatiently, I went
Careening down. December is a place

I revisit every year: a set of keeled
And flaking apparatus, parked on grey
Midwinter tarmac—seesaw, swings, the chute
Clogged with leafscraps sodden as congealed
Cornflakes. A lanky, scissoring midday
Shadow stalks before me as I scoot

To make the roundabout before it wheels
Faster than I can mount. I slither, sick
With effort, across the web, manhandled by
A clutch of skinny kids. The month unreels
Itself with the blurred horizon as we pick
Up caterwauling speed. December sky

Flickers its permutations—ravelling wool
Snagged on a glinting chip of sun; a pall
Of gaberdine; a nursery high tea
Of flaked fish on a blue plate—till the pull
Unclamps my fingers from the wheel; I fall,
Giddy, on grit-stung palms and knees, to see

Snow falling from a doughy and impassive
Sky—sinking, rising in perspective, slack
As the third day after Boxing Day. The ride
Done . . . though the roundabout still turns with massive
Snowlike momentum. Chalklines highlight black
Revolving spokes. I dust myself off, stride
Through playground gates to the blank sheet of New Year.

COLIN ROWBOTHAM

Orchids

They lean over the path,
Adder-mouthed,
Swaying close to the face,
Coming out, soft and deceptive,
Limp and damp, delicate as a young bird's tongue;
Their fluttery fledgeling lips
Move slowly,
Drawing in the warm air.

And at night,
The faint moon falling through whitewashed glass,
The heat going down
So their musky smell comes even stronger,
Drifting down from their mossy cradles:
So many devouring infants!
Soft luminescent fingers,
Lips neither dead nor alive,
Loose ghostly mouths
Breathing.

THEODORE ROETHKE

Waterfall

The burn drowns steadily in its own downpour,
A helter-skelter of muslin and glass
That skids to a halt, crashing up suds.

Simultaneous acceleration
And sudden braking; water goes over
Like villains dropped screaming to justice.

It appears an athletic glacier
Has reared into reverse: is swallowed up
And regurgitated through this long throat.

My eye rides over and downwards, falls with
Hurtling tons that slabber and spill,
Falls, yet records the tumult thus standing still.

SEAMUS HEANEY

The Forge

All I know is a door into the dark.
Outside, old axles and iron hoops rusting;
Inside, the hammered anvil's short-pitched ring,
The unpredictable fantail of sparks
Or hiss when a new shoe toughens in water.
The anvil must be somewhere in the centre,
Horned as a unicorn, at one end square,
Set there immovable: an altar
Where he expends himself in shape and music.
Sometimes, leather-aproned, hairs in his nose,
He leans out on the jamb, recalls a clatter
Of hoofs where traffic is flashing in rows;
Then grunts and goes in, with a slam and flick
To beat real iron out, to work the bellows.

SEAMUS HEANEY

Storm on the Island

We are prepared: we build our houses squat,
Sink walls in rock and roof them with good slate.
This wizened earth has never troubled us
With hay, so, as you see, there are no stacks
Or stooks that can be lost. Nor are there trees
Which might prove company when it blows full
Blast: you know what I mean—leaves and branches
Can raise a tragic chorus in a gale
So that you listen to the thing you fear
Forgetting that it pummels your house too.
But there are no trees, no natural shelter.
You might think that the sea is company,
Exploding comfortably down on the cliffs
But no: when it begins, the flung spray hits
The very windows, spits like a tame cat
Turned savage. We just sit tight while wind dives
And strafes invisibly. Space is a salvo,
We are bombarded by the empty air.
Strange, it is a huge nothing that we fear.

SEAMUS HEANEY

Laundrette

We sit nebulous in steam.
It calms the air and makes the windows stream
rippling the hinterland's big houses to a blur
of bedsits—not a patch on what they were before.

We stuff the tub, jam money in the slot,
sit back on rickle chairs not
reading. The paperbacks in our pockets curl.
Our eyes are riveted. Our own colours whirl.

We pour in smithereens of soap. The machine sobs
through its cycle. The rhythm throbs
and changes. Suds drool and slobber in the churn.
Our duds don't know which way to turn.

The dark shoves one man in,
lugging a bundle like a wandering Jew. Linen
washed in public here.
We let out of the bag who we are.

This youngwife has a fine stack of sheets, each pair
a present. She admires their clean cut air
of colourschemes and being chosen. Are the dyes fast?
This christening lather will be the first test.

This woman is deadpan before the rinse and sluice
of the family in a bagwash. Let them stew in their juice
to a final fankle, twisted, wrung out into rope,
hard to unravel. She sees a kaleidoscope

For her to narrow her eyes and blow smoke at, his overalls
and pants ballooning, tangling with her smalls
and the teeshirts skinned from her wriggling son.
She has a weather eye for what might shrink or run.

This dour man does for himself. Before him,
half lost, his small possessions swim.
Cast off, random
they nose and nudge the porthole glass like flotsam.

LIZ LOCHHEAD

Bendix

This porthole overlooks a sea
Forever falling from the sky,
The water inextricably
Involved with buttons, suds and dye.

Like bits of shrapnel, shards of foam
Fly heavenward; a bedsheet heaves,
A stocking wrestles with a comb,
And cotton angels wave their sleeves.

The boiling purgatorial tide
Revolves our dreary shorts and slips,
While Mother coolly bakes beside
Her little jugged apocalypse.

JOHN UPDIKE

The Place's Fault

Once, after a rotten day at school—
Sweat on my fingers, pages thumbed with smears,
Cane smashing down to make me keep them neat—
I blinked out to the sunlight and the heat
And stumbled up the hill, still swallowing tears.
A stone hissed past my ear—'Yah! gurt fat fool!'

Some urchins waited for me by my gate.
I shouted swear-words at them, walked away.
'Yeller,' they yelled, 'e's yeller!' And they flung
Clods, stones, bricks—anything to make me run.
I ran, all right, up hill all summer day
With 'yeller' in my ears. 'I'm not, I'm not!'

Another time, playing too near the shops—
Oddly, no doubt, I'm told I was quite odd,
Making, no doubt, a noise—a girl in slacks
Came out and told some kids 'Run round the back,
Bash in his back door, smash up his back yard,
And if he yells I'll go and fetch the cops.'

And what a rush I had to lock those doors
Before that rabble reached them! What desire
I've had these twenty years to lock away
That place where fingers pointed out my play,
Where even the grass was tangled with barbed wire,
Where through the streets I waged continual wars!

We left (it was a temporary halt)
The knots of ragged kids, the wired-off beach,
Faces behind the blinds. I'll not return;
There's nothing there I haven't had to learn,
And I've learned nothing that I'd care to teach—
Except that I know it was the place's fault.

PHILIP HOBSBAUM

★ **Poster poems.** Many of the poems in this section have vividly descriptive lines or phrases—'the rain's dragging grey columns / Smudged the farms' (*November*, p. 131); orchids that are 'adder-mouthed' (p. 135); a waterfall that looks as if 'an athletic glacier / Has reared into reverse' (p. 136). There are many more. Choose one poem that appeals to you and design a poster to illustrate it, including one or two lines to go with your picture, either as a caption or as part of the design.

★ **Places.** There are several word-pictures of particular places here—a depressing park in an industrial area (p. 130), the Thames embankment in winter (p. 140), a forge (p. 137) and a laundrette (p. 138). Choose two or three of the poems to read; then talk about which poem makes you *see* the place most clearly in your mind's eye.

Then, hear *The Place's Fault* (p. 142) and *Not from here* (p. 141) read aloud. What are these two poems saying about people and places? (John la Rose is a Trinidadian poet.)

Finally, on your own, list as many details as you can of a particular place that is important to you. From your list, make your own word-picture.

★ **Machines.** *Bendix* (p. 139) combines some clever images within a neat, regular form. Read it aloud and talk about the images, rhyme and rhythm. Working in pairs, try to do the same for other domestic objects—using a lawnmower, hoovering, using a food mixer, a sewing machine.

Satires and Opinions

Meditatio

When I carefully consider the curious habits of dogs
I am compelled to conclude
That man is the superior animal.

When I consider the curious habits of man
I confess, my friend, I am puzzled.

EZRA POUND

Animals

I think I could turn and live with animals, they are so placid and
    self-contain'd,
I stand and look at them long and long.

They do not sweat and whine about their condition,
They do not lie awake in the dark and weep for their sins,
They do not make me sick discussing their duty to God,
Not one is dissatisfied, not one is demented with the mania of
    owning things,
Not one kneels to another, nor to his kind that lived thousands
    of years ago,
Not one is respectable or unhappy over the whole earth.

WALT WHITMAN

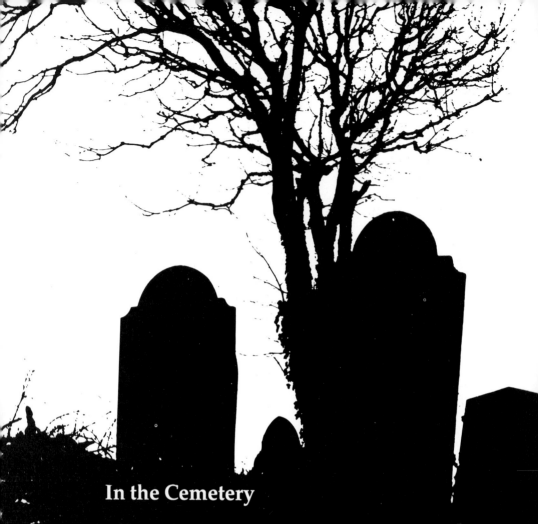

In the Cemetery

'You see those mothers squabbling there?'
Remarks the man of the cemetery.
'One says in tears, *"Tis mine lies here!"*
Another, *"Nay, mine, you Pharisee!"*
Another, *"How dare you move my flowers*
And put your own on this grave of ours!"
But all their children were laid therein
At different times, like sprats in a tin.

'And then the main drain had to cross,
And we moved the lot some nights ago,
And packed them away in the general foss
With hundreds more. But their folks don't know,
And as well cry over a new-laid drain
As anything else, to ease your pain!'

THOMAS HARDY

In Church

'And now to God the Father', he ends,
And his voice thrills up to the topmost tiles:
Each listener chokes as he bows and bends,
And emotion pervades the crowded aisles.
Then the preacher glides to the vestry-door,
And shuts it, and thinks he is seen no more.

The door swings softly ajar meanwhile,
And a pupil of his in the Bible class,
Who adores him as one without gloss or guile,
Sees her idol stand with a satisfied smile
And re-enact at the vestry-glass
Each pulpit gesture in deft dumb-show
That had moved the congregation so.

THOMAS HARDY

In Westminster Abbey

Let me take this other glove off
    As the vox humana swells,
And the beauteous fields of Eden
    Bask beneath the Abbey bells.
Here, where England's statesmen lie,
Listen to a lady's cry.

Gracious Lord, oh bomb the Germans.
    Spare their women for Thy Sake,
And if that is not too easy
    We will pardon Thy Mistake.
But, Gracious Lord, whate'er shall be,
Don't let anyone bomb me.

Keep our Empire undismembered
    Guide our Forces by Thy Hand,
Gallant blacks from far Jamaica,
    Honduras and Togoland;
Protect them Lord in all their fights,
And, even more, protect the whites.

Think of what our Nation stands for,
    Books from Boots' and country lanes,
Free speech, free passes, class distinction,
    Democracy and proper drains.
Lord, put beneath Thy special care
One-eighty-nine Cadogan Square.

Although dear Lord I am a sinner,
    I have done no major crime;
Now I'll come to Evening Service
    Whensoever I have the time.
So, Lord, reserve for me a crown,
And do not let my shares go down.

I will labour for Thy Kingdom,
    Help our lads to win the war,
Send white feathers to the cowards
    Join the Women's Army Corps,
Then wash the Steps around Thy Throne
In the Eternal Safety Zone.

Now I feel a little better,
    What a treat to hear Thy Word,
Where the bones of leading statesmen,
    Have so often been interr'd.
And now, dear Lord, I cannot wait
Because I have a luncheon date.

                    JOHN BETJEMAN

Back In The Playground Blues

I dreamed I was back in the playground, I was about four feet
   high
Yes dreamed I was back in the playground, standing about four
   feet high
Well the playground was three miles long and the playground
   was five miles wide

It was broken black tarmac with a high wire fence all around
Broken black dusty tarmac with a high fence running all around
And it had a special name to it, they called it The Killing Ground

Got a mother and a father, they're one thousand years away
The rulers of The Killing Ground are coming out to play
Everybody thinking: "Who they going to play with today?"

   Well you get it for being Jewish
   And you get it for being black
   Get it for being chicken
   And you get it for fighting back
   You get it for being big and fat
   Get it for being small
   Oh those who get it get it and get it
   For any damn thing at all

Sometimes they take a beetle, tear off its six legs one by one
Beetle on its black back, rocking in the lunchtime sun
But a beetle can't beg for mercy, a beetle's not half the fun

I heard a deep voice talking, it had that iceberg sound
"It prepares them for Life"—but I have never found
Any place in my life worse than The Killing Ground.

ADRIAN MITCHELL

For Heidi with Blue Hair

When you dyed your hair blue
(or, at least, ultramarine
for the clipped sides, with a crest
of jet-black spikes on top)
you were sent home from school

because, as the headmistress put it,
although dyed hair was not
specifically forbidden, yours
was, apart from anything else,
not done in the school colours.

Tears in the kitchen, telephone-calls
to school from your freedom-loving father:
'She's not a punk in her behaviour;
it's just a style.' (You wiped your eyes,
also not in a school colour.)

'She discussed it with me first—
we checked the rules.' 'And anyway, Dad,
it cost twenty-five dollars.
Tell them it won't wash out—not even if I
    wanted to try.'

It would have been unfair to mention
your mother's death, but that
shimmered behind the arguments.
The school had nothing else against you;
the teachers twittered and gave in.

Next day your black friend had hers done
in grey, white and flaxen yellow—
the school colours precisely:
an act of solidarity, a witty
tease. The battle was already won.

FLEUR ADCOCK

The Lesson

A tree enters and says with a bow:
    I am a tree.
A black tear falls from the sky and says:
    I am a bird.

Down a spider's web
    something like love
        comes near
            and says:
    I am silence.

But by the blackboard sprawls
    a national democratic
    horse in his waistcoat
    and repeats,
    pricking his ears on every side,
    repeats and repeats
        I am the engine of history
        and
        we all
        love
        progress
        and
        courage
        and
        the fighters' wrath.

Under the classroom door
trickles
a thin stream of blood.

For here begins
the massacre
of the innocents.

MIROSLAV HOLUB
(*trans. I. Milner and G. Theiner*)

The Home Front

Father mows the lawn and Mother peels the potatoes
Grandma lays the table alone,
And adjusts a photograph of the unknown soldier
In this Holy of Holies, the Home.
And from the TV an unwatched voice
Suggests the answer is to plant more trees,
The scrawl on the wall says what about the workers
And the voice of the people says more salt please.

Mother shakes her head and reads aloud from the newspaper
As Father puts another lock on the door,
And reflects upon the violent times that we are living in
While chatting with the wife beater next door.
If paradise to you is cheap beer and overtime
Home truths are easily missed,
Something that every football fan knows
It only takes five fingers to form a fist.

And when it rains here
It rains so hard
But never hard enough to wash away the sorrow.
I'll trade my love today for a greater love tomorrow.
The lonely child looks out and dreams of independence
From this family life sentence.

Mother sees but does not read the peeling posters
And can't believe that there's a world to be won,
But in the public schools and in the public houses
The Battle of Britain goes on.
The constant promise of jam tomorrow
Is the New Breed's litany and verse,
If it takes another war to fill the churches of England
Then the world the meek inherit, what will it be worth?

Mother fights the tears and Father his sense of outrage
And attempts to justify the sacrifice,
To pass their creed down to another generation
'Anything for the quiet life'.
In the Land of A Thousand Doses
Where nostalgia is the opium of the age,
Our place in History is as
Clock watchers, old timers, window shoppers.

BILLY BRAGG

All-Purpose Poem for State Occasions

The nation rejoices or mourns
As this happy or sombre day dawns.
Our eyes will be wet
As we sit round the set,
Neglecting our flowerbeds and lawns.

As Her Majesty rides past the crowd
They'll be silent or cheer very loud
But whatever they do
It's undoubtedly true
That they'll feel patriotic and proud.

In Dundee and Penzance and Ealing
We're imbued with appropriate feeling:
We're British and loyal
And love every royal
And tonight we shall drink till we're reeling.

WENDY COPE

A Consumer's Report

The name of the product I tested is LIFE.
I have completed the form you sent me
and understand that my answers are confidential.

I had it as a gift,
I didn't feel much while using it,
in fact, I think I'd have liked to be more excited.
It seemed gentle on the hands
but left an embarrassing deposit behind.
It was not economical
and I have used much more than I thought
(I suppose I have about half left
but it's difficult to tell)—
Although the instructions are fairly large
there are so many of them
I don't know which to follow, especially
as they seem to contradict each other.
I'm not sure such a thing
should be put in the way of children
(heaven knows they're growing up
quickly enough already);
it's difficult to think of a purpose
for it. One of my friends says
it's just to keep its maker in a job.
Also the price is much too high.
Things are piling up so fast,
after all, the world got by
for a thousand million years
without this, do we need it now?
(Incidentally, please ask your man
to stop calling me 'the respondent';
I don't like the sound of it.)
There seem to be a lot of different labels,
sizes and colours should be uniform,
the shape is awkward, it's waterproof
but not heat-resistant, it doesn't keep
yet it's very difficult to get rid of.
Whenever they make it cheaper they seem
to put less in: if you say you don't
want it, then it's delivered anyway—

I'd agree it's a popular product,
it's got into the language; people
even say they're on the side of it.
Personally I think it's overdone,
a small thing people are ready
to behave badly about. I think
we should take it for granted. If its
experts are called philosophers or market
researchers or historians, we shouldn't
care. We are the consumers and the last
law makers. So finally, I'd buy it.
But the question of a 'best buy'
I'd like to leave until I get
the competitive product you said you'd send.

PETER PORTER

What Did You Learn in School Today?

What did you learn in school today, dear little boy of mine?
What did you learn in school today, dear little boy of mine?

1. I learned that Washington never told a lie;
   I learned that soldiers seldom die;
   I learned that everybody's free,
   And that's what the teacher said to me.
   And that's what I learned in school today
   That's what I learned in school.

2. I learned that policemen are my friends,
   I learned that justice never ends,
   I learned that murderers die for their crimes,
   Even if we make a mistake sometimes.

3. I learned our government must be strong,
   It's always right and never wrong,
   Our leaders are the finest men,
   And we elect 'em again and again.

4. I learned that war is not so bad,
   I learned about the great ones we have had,
   We fought in Germany and in France,
   And someday I might get my chance.

TOM PAXTON

Imagine

Imagine there's no heaven
It's easy if you try.
No hell below us,
Above us only sky.
Imagine all the people,
Living for today.

Imagine there's no countries
It isn't hard to do,
Nothing to kill or die for
And no religion too.
Imagine all the people
Living life in peace.
You may say I'm a dreamer,
But I'm not the only one.
I hope some day you'll join us
And the world will be as one.

Imagine no possessions
I wonder if you can,
No need for greed or hunger
A brotherhood of man.
Imagine all the people
Sharing all the world.
You may say I'm a dreamer,
But I'm not the only one.
I hope some day you'll join us
And the world will live as one.

JOHN LENNON

The Big Rock Candy Mountains

One evenin' as the sun went down
And the jungle fire was burnin',
Down the track came a hobo hikin',
And he said: 'Boys, I'm not turnin',
I'm headed fer a land that's far away
Beside the crystal fountains,
So come with me, we'll all go see
The Big Rock Candy Mountains.'

In the Big Rock Candy Mountains,
There's a land that's fair and bright,
Where the handouts grow on bushes,
And you sleep out every night.
Where the boxcars are all empty,
And the sun shines every day
On the birds and the bees and the cigarette trees,
And the lemonade springs where the bluebird sings,
In the Big Rock Candy Mountains.

In the Big Rock Candy Mountains,
All the cops have wooden legs,
The bulldogs all have rubber teeth,
And the hens lay soft-boiled eggs,
The farmer's trees are full of fruit,
And the barns are full of hay.
Oh, I'm bound to go where there ain't no snow,
Where the rain don't pour, the wind don't blow,
In the Big Rock Candy Mountains.

In the Big Rock Candy Mountains,
You never change your socks,
And the little streams of alcohol
Come tricklin' down the rocks.
There the brakemen have to tip their hats
And the railroad bulls are blind.
There's a lake of stew and of whisky too,
You can paddle all around 'em in a big canoe,
In the Big Rock Candy Mountains.

In the Big Rock Candy Mountains,
All the jails are made of tin,
And you can bust right out again
As soon as you are in.
There ain't no short-handled shovels,
No axes, saws or picks.
I'm goin' to stay where you sleep all day,
Where they hung the Turk that invented work,
In the Big Rock Candy Mountains.

ANON.

Once

Once they gave a smile
& called me ethnic

once they looked amazed
& called me kinetic

once they applauded
& called me magic

now they say get out from under there
we know you're hiding under that stick
come out now or we'll shoot you hear

JOHN AGARD

I Like That Stuff

Lovers lie around in it.
Broken glass is found in it
Grass
I like that stuff

Tuna fish get wrapped in it
Legs come wrapped in it
Nylon
I like that stuff

Eskimos and tramps chew it
Madame Tussaud gave status to it
Wax
I like that stuff

Elephants get sprayed with it
Scotch is made with it
Water
I like that stuff

Clergy are dumbfounded by it
Bones are surrounded by it
Flesh
I like that stuff

Harps are strung with it
Mattresses are sprung with it
Wire
I like that stuff

Cigarettes are lit by it
Pensioners get happy when they sit by it
Fire
I like that stuff

Dankworth's alto is made of it, most of it,
Scoobdedoo is composed of it
Plastic
I like that stuff

Man made fibres and raw materials
Old rolled gold and breakfast cereals
Platinum linoleum
I like that stuff

Skin on my hands
Hair on my head
Toenails on my feet
And linen on my bed

Well I like that stuff
Yes I like that stuff
   The earth
Is made of earth
   And I like that stuff

ADRIAN MITCHELL

161

162

next to of course god america i

'next to of course god america i
love you land of the pilgrims' and so forth oh
say can you see by the dawn's early my
country 'tis of centuries come and go
and are no more what of it we should worry
in every language even deafanddumb
thy sons acclaim your glorious name by gorry
by jingo by gee by gosh by gum
why talk of beauty what could be more beautiful than these heroic happy dead
who rushed like lions to the roaring slaughter
they did not stop to think they died instead
then shall the voice of liberty be mute?'

He spoke. And drank rapidly a glass of water

e. e. cummings

Stereotype

I'm a fullblooded
West Indian stereotype
See me straw hat?
Watch it good

I'm a fullblooded
West Indian stereotype
You ask
if I got riddum
in me blood
You going ask!
Man just beat de drum
and don't forget
to pour de rum

I'm a fullblooded
West Indian stereotype
You say
I suppose you can show
us the limbo, can't you?

How you know!
How you know!
You sure
you don't want me
sing you a calypso too
How about that

I'm a fullblooded
West Indian stereotype
You call me
happy-go-lucky
Yes that's me
dressing fancy
and chasing woman
if you think ah lie
bring yuh sister

I'm a fullblooded
West Indian stereotype
You wonder
where do you people
get such riddum
could it be the sunshine
My goodness
just listen to that steelband

Isn't there one thing
you forgot to ask
go on man ask ask
This native will answer anything
How about cricket?
I suppose you're good at it?
Hear this man
good at it!
Put de willow
in me hand
and watch me stripe
de boundary

Yes I'm a fullblooded
West Indian stereotype

that's why I
graduated from Oxford University
with a degree
in anthropology

JOHN AGARD

Once Upon A Time

Once upon a time, son,
they used to laugh with their hearts
and laugh with their eyes;
but now they only laugh with their teeth,
while their ice-block-cold eyes
search behind my shadow.

There was a time indeed
they used to shake hands with their hearts;
but that's gone, son.
Now they shake hands without hearts
while their left hands search
my empty pockets.

"Feel at home," "Come again,"
they say, and when I come
again and feel
at home, once, twice,
there will be no thrice—
for then I find doors shut on me.

So I have learned many things, son.
I have learned to wear many faces
like dresses—homeface,
officeface, streetface, hostface, cock-
tailface, with all their conforming smiles
like a fixed portrait smile.

And I have learned too
to laugh with only my teeth
and shake hands without my heart.
I have also learned to say, "Goodbye,"
when I mean "Goodriddance";
to say "Glad to meet you,"
without being glad; and to say "It's been
nice talking to you," after being bored.

But believe me, son.
I want to be what I used to be
when I was like you. I want
to unlearn all these muting things.
Most of all, I want to relearn
how to laugh, for my laugh in the mirror
shows only my teeth like a snake's bare fangs!

So show me, son,
how to laugh; show me how
I used to laugh and smile
once upon a time when I was like you.

GABRIEL OKARA

The Projectionist's Nightmare

This is the projectionist's nightmare:
A bird finds its way into the cinema,
finds the beam, flies down it,
smashes into a screen depicting a garden,
a sunset and two people being nice to each other.
Real blood, real intestines, slither down
the likeness of a tree.
'This is no good,' screams the audience,
'This is not what we came to see.'

BRIAN PATTEN

When I Went to the Film

When I went to the film, and saw all the black-and-white feelings
    that nobody felt,
and heard the audience sighing and sobbing with all the
    emotions they none of them felt,
and saw them cuddling with rising passions they none of them
    for a moment felt,
and caught them moaning from close-up kisses, black-and-white
    kisses that could not be felt,
it was like being in heaven, which I am sure has a white
    atmosphere
upon which shadows of people, pure personalities
are cast in black and white, and move
in flat ecstasy, supremely unfelt,
and heavenly.

D. H. LAWRENCE

★ **Performances.** Many of the poems in this section are ideal for performing in pairs or small groups. It is possible to take a set of poems that are linked in some way and to make a tape recording of them.

Holy Ground
—Thomas Hardy's poem, *In the Cemetery*, on page 146 can be read by four people each taking the part of one of the mothers or the narrator.
—John Betjeman's poem, *In Westminster Abbey*, is a performance for only one voice. It needs to be read in the refined and rather exaggerated tones of an upper class lady.

The Killing Ground
—*Back In The Playground Blues* by Adrian Mitchell can be divided up among several different voices. You may find it helps to get a feel for the rhythm and movement of this style of talking blues if you listen to other examples on record.
—A poem that makes an appropriate pair to the one by Adrian Mitchell is Tom Paxton's *What Did You Learn in School Today?* where question and reply can be taken by different voices.
—Fleur Adcock's poem on page 150 about the occasion when her god-daughter, Heidi, dyed her hair blue can be dramatised by two or three readers.
—Miroslav Holub's poem *The Lesson* on page 151 can easily and effectively be shared among several voices.

Home Ground
—The words of Billy Bragg's song *The Home Front* can be read by several different voices. You may find it helpful to split each of the eight line verses into two sets of four lines.
—*All-Purpose Poem for State Occasions* by Wendy Cope might make a suitable companion to the Billy Bragg piece.
—At first glance, Peter Porter's Poem *A Consumer's Report* might look as though it can only be read by one voice but you can divide it up quite effectively if you think carefully about where the breaks should come. Try writing your own Consumer's Report about the 'competitive product' that is referred to in the last line.

168

* **Utopian Dreams?** John Lennon's song *Imagine* describes an ideal world of spiritual peace and harmony. The traditional song about the wonderful land of *The Big Rock Candy Mountains* is much more concerned with the pleasures of the flesh. Perhaps we all dream about Utopia—our own perfect land. If you have an idea of *your* Utopia try to capture something of it in verse. You could continue either of these songs with your own material.

  —In a similar vein, you could, after reading Adrian Mitchell's poem *I Like That Stuff* on page 160, list the things you like and, using the same verse pattern, continue the poem with your own favourite things. Alternatively, of course, you could write a piece which is the exact opposite—*I Hate that Stuff!*

* **Patriotic Patter.** e. e. cummings' poem on page 163 with the odd title of *next to of course god america i* contains in every line at least one cliché of the kind that is so often spouted by politicians. The clichés are nearly all drawn from patriotic songs, speeches, and verse and are crammed together in a mad jumble only stopping at the next to last line. The whole inflated balloon is then punctured. In pairs, make a list of any similar clichés you might find in newspaper headlines, political speeches, rousing songs and so forth . . . 'Land of . . .' 'tighten our belts . . .' 'We must all pull together . . .' and so on. Try to weave them into a piece on the same pattern as cummings' poem. Join forces with another pair if you need more ideas. The poem is, almost unbelievably, a sonnet! (see p. 47)

* **Stereotypes.** John Agard was born in Guyana in the Caribbean and now lives in Britain. In his poem *Stereotype* he pokes gentle fun at the way in which some people in Britain view him. Because he is of black Caribbean origin he must, they reason, therefore be a calypso singing, limbo dancing, cricket lover and so on. It's rather like somebody meeting an average British male and expecting him to wear a bowler hat, a pin-stripe suit and carry an umbrella—to be a stereotype Briton, in fact. Work out a reading of the poem as a group performance and tape it. What other stereotypes can you think of? What are the stereotype football fans, teachers, skinheads . . . ? Work in pairs to list some of your ideas about one stereotype and then try to write, either singly or together, a similar piece to John Agard's poem.

War

The Rear-Guard

(Hindenburg Line, April 1917)

Groping along the tunnel, step by step,
He winked his prying torch with patching glare
From side to side, and sniffed the unwholesome air.

Tins, boxes, bottles, shapes too vague to know;
A mirror smashed, the mattress from a bed;
And he, exploring fifty feet below
The rosy gloom of battle overhead.

Tripping, he grabbed the wall; saw some one lie
Humped at his feet, half-hidden by a rug,
And stooped to give the sleeper's arm a tug.
'I'm looking for headquarters.' No reply.
'God blast your neck!' (For days he'd had no sleep,)
'Get up and guide me through this stinking place.'

Savage, he kicked a soft, unanswering heap,
And flashed his beam across the livid face
Terribly glaring up, whose eyes yet wore
Agony dying hard ten days before;
And fists of fingers clutched a blackening wound.

Alone he staggered on until he found
Dawn's ghost that filtered down a shafted stair
To the dazed, muttering creatures underground
Who hear the boom of shells in muffled sound.
At last, with sweat of horror in his hair,
He climbed through darkness to the twilight air,
Unloading hell behind him step by step.

SIEGFRIED SASSOON

170

Christmas: 1924

'Peace upon earth!' was said. We sing it,
And pay a million priests to bring it.
After two thousand years of mass
We've got as far as poison gas.

THOMAS HARDY

The Dead-Beat

He dropped,—more sullenly than wearily,
Lay stupid like a cod, heavy like meat,
And none of us could kick him to his feet;
Just blinked at my revolver, blearily;
—Didn't appear to know a war was on,
Or see the blasted trench at which he stared.
'I'll do 'em in,' he whined. 'If this hand's spared,
I'll murder them, I will.'

                A low voice said,
'It's Blighty, p'raps, he sees; his pluck's all gone,
Dreaming of all the valiant, that aren't dead:
Bold uncles, smiling ministerially;
Maybe his brave young wife, getting her fun
In some new home, improved materially.
It's not these stiffs have crazed him; nor the Hun.'

We sent him down at last, out of the way.
Unwounded;—stout lad, too, before that strafe.
Malingering? Stretcher-bearers winked, 'Not half!'

Next day I heard the Doc.'s well-whiskied laugh:
'That scum you sent last night soon died. Hooray.'

WILFRED OWEN

171

The Hero

'Jack fell as he'd have wished,' the Mother said,
And folded up the letter that she'd read.
'The Colonel writes so nicely.' Something broke
In the tired voice that quavered to a choke.
She half looked up. 'We mothers are so proud
Of our dead soldiers.' Then her face was bowed.

Quietly the Brother Officer went out.
He'd told the poor old dear some gallant lies
That she would nourish all her days, no doubt.
For while he coughed and mumbled, her weak eyes
Had shone with gentle triumph, brimmed with joy,
Because he'd been so brave, her glorious boy.

He thought how 'Jack', cold-footed, useless swine,
Had panicked down the trench that night the mine
Went up at Wicked Corner; how he'd tried
To get sent home, and how, at last, he died,
Blown to small bits. And no one seemed to care
Except that lonely woman with white hair.

SIEGFRIED SASSOON

High Wood

Ladies and gentlemen, this is High Wood,
Called by the French, Bois des Fourneaux,
The famous spot which in Nineteen-Sixteen,
July, August and September was the scene
Of long and bitterly contested strife,
By reason of its High commanding site.
Observe the effect of shell-fire in the trees.
Standing and fallen; here is wire; this trench
For months inhabited, twelve times changed hands;
(They soon fall in), used later as a grave.
It has been said on good authority
That in the fighting for this patch of wood
Were killed somewhere above eight thousand men,
Of whom the greater part were buried here,
This mound on which you stand being . . .
                                        Madame, please,

You are requested kindly not to touch
Or take away the Company's property
As souvenirs; you'll find we have on sale
A large variety, all guaranteed.
As I was saying, all is as it was,
This is an unknown British officer,
The tunic having lately rotted off.
Please follow me—this way . . .
                            the *path*, sir, *please*,
The ground which was secured at great expense
The Company keeps absolutely untouched,
And in that dug-out (genuine) we provide
Refreshments at a reasonable rate.
You are requested not to leave about
Paper, or ginger-beer bottles, or orange-peel,
There are waste-paper baskets at the gate.

PHILIP JOHNSTONE

Dulce et Decorum Est

[handwritten annotation: long, with commas]

Bent double, like old beggars under sacks,
Knock-kneed, coughing like hags, we cursed through sludge,
Till on the haunting flares we turned our backs,
And towards our distant rest began to trudge.
Men marched asleep. Many had lost their boots,
But limped on, blood-shod. All went lame, all blind;
Drunk with fatigue; deaf even to the hoots
Of gas-shells dropping softly behind.

Gas! GAS! Quick, boys!—An ecstasy of fumbling, *[handwritten annotation: — dashes! to show panic.]*
Fitting the clumsy helmets just in time,
But someone still was yelling out and stumbling
And floundering like a man in fire or lime.—
Dim through the misty panes and thick green light,
As under a green sea, I saw him drowning.

In all my dreams before my helpless sight
He plunges at me, guttering, choking, drowning. *[handwritten annotation: — Climax]*

[handwritten annotation: pointing finger]

If in some smothering dreams, you too could pace
Behind the wagon that we flung him in,
And watch the white eyes writhing in his face,
His hanging face, like a devil's sick of sin;
If you could hear at every jolt, the blood
Come gargling from the froth-corrupted lungs,
Bitter as the cud
Of vile, incurable sores on innocent tongues,—
My friend, you would not tell with such high zest
To children ardent for some desperate glory,
The old Lie: *Dulce et decorum est*
Pro patria mori.

                                        WILFRED OWEN

All Day It Has Rained

All day it has rained, and we on the edge of the moors
Have sprawled in our bell-tents, moody and dull as boors,
Groundsheets and blankets spread on the muddy ground
And from the first grey wakening we have found
No refuge from the skirmishing fine rain
And the wind that made the canvas heave and flap
And the taut wet guy-ropes ravel out and snap.
All day the rain has glided, wave and mist and dream,
Drenching the gorse and heather, a gossamer stream
Too light to stir the acorns that suddenly
Snatched from their cups by the wild south-westerly
Pattered against the tent and our upturned dreaming faces.
And we stretched out, unbuttoning our braces,
Smoking a Woodbine, darning dirty socks,
Reading the Sunday papers—I saw a fox
And mentioned it in the note I scribbled home;—
And we talked of girls and dropping bombs on Rome, ·
And thought of the quiet dead and the loud celebrities
Exhorting us to slaughter, and the herded refugees;
—Yet thought softly, morosely of them, and as indifferently
As of ourselves or those whom we
For years have loved, and will again
Tomorrow maybe love; but now it is the rain
Possesses us entirely, the twilight and the rain.

And I can remember nothing dearer or more to my heart
Than the children I watched in the woods on Saturday
Shaking down burning chestnuts for the schoolyard's merry
    play,
Or the shaggy patient dog who followed me
By Sheet and Steep and up the wooded scree
To the Shoulder o' Mutton where Edward Thomas brooded long
On death and beauty—till a bullet stopped his song.

ALUN LEWIS

The Soldier

love sonnet to England.

8 lines explaining the situation

If I should die, think only this of me:
    That there's some corner of a foreign field
That is for ever England. There shall be
    In that rich earth a richer dust concealed;
A dust whom England bore, shaped, made aware,
    Gave, once, her flowers to love, her ways to roam,
A body of England's, breathing English air,
    Washed by the rivers, blest by suns of home.

repeating England.

6 lines reflection.

And think, this heart, all evil shed away,
    A pulse in the eternal mind, no less
        Gives somewhere back the thoughts by England given;
Her sights and sounds; dreams happy as her day;
    And laughter, learnt of friends; and gentleness,
        In hearts at peace, under an English heaven.

RUPERT BROOKE

177

Todes Meer

By Paul Nash, 1940–1
(Dead Sea)

1

This picture is of waste. No victory
gloats in the absent eye that we make ours
by seeing what it saw. But tragedy
is not stressed either; we may keep our tears.

No beggar whimpers for them, we are shown
no scars, no mutilations, no burnt boys
but, bleached by moonlight, aircraft wreckage thrown
into an open grave for broken toys.

An Icarus has fallen from the sky.
Another and another fall, a rain
of torches must have fallen. This clear eye
records the waste, does not insist on pain.

Pity witheld is power; a reservoir
of weeping gathers, war-dammed in the brain.

2

The time is dawn. The moon
hangs on withdrawing dark
shedding just light enough
to cast shadows that mark
the sand. On ragged waves—
as rigid in arrest
as signpost dead—each crest
postures as though it lives,
threatens but cannot reach
with more than shadow-claws
the dead sea's desert beach:
yet this dry tide still gnaws
the fields away; lost land
submerges, all but drowned.

ANNA ADAMS

Judging Distances

Not only how far away, but the way that you say it
Is very important. Perhaps you may never get
The knack of judging a distance, but at least you know
How to report on a landscape: the central sector,
The right of arc and that, which we had last Tuesday,
    And at least you know

That maps are of time, not place, so far as the army
Happens to be concerned—the reason being,
Is one which need not delay us. Again, you know
There are three kinds of tree, three only, the fir and the poplar,
And those which have bushy tops to; and lastly
    That things only seem to be things.

A barn is not called a barn, to put it more plainly,
Or a field in the distance, where sheep may be safely grazing.
You must never be over-sure. You must say, when reporting:
At five o'clock in the central sector is a dozen
Of what appear to be animals; whatever you do,
      Don't call the bleeders *sheep*.

I am sure that's quite clear; and suppose, for the sake of
    example,
The one at the end, asleep, endeavours to tell us
What he sees over there to the west, and how far away,
After first having come to attention. There to the west,
On the fields of summer the sun and the shadows bestow
      Vestments of purple and gold.

The still white dwellings are like a mirage in the heat,
And under the swaying elms a man and a woman
Lie gently together. Which is, perhaps, only to say
That there is a row of houses to the left of arc,
And that under some poplars a pair of what appear to be
    humans
      Appear to be loving.

Well that, for an answer, is what we might rightly call
Moderately satisfactory only, the reason being,
Is that two things have been omitted, and those are important.
The human beings, now: in what direction are they,
And how far away, would you say? And do not forget
      There may be dead ground in between.

There may be dead ground in between; and I may not have got
The knack of judging a distance; I will only venture
A guess that perhaps between me and the apparent lovers,
(Who, incidentally, appear by now to have finished),
At seven o' clock from the houses, is roughly a distance
      Of about one year and a half.

HENRY REED

Survivors

With the ship burning in their eyes
The white faces float like refuse
In the darkness—the water screwing
Oily circles where the hot steel lies.

They clutch with fingers frozen into claws
The lifebelts thrown from a destroyer,
And see, between the future's doors,
The gasping entrance of the sea.

Taken on board as many as lived, who
Had a mind left for living and the ocean,
They open eyes running with surf,
Heavy with the grey ghosts of explosion.

The meaning is not yet clear,
Where daybreak died in the smile—
And the mouth remained stiff
And grinning, stupid for a little while.

But soon they joke, easy and warm,
As men will who have died once
Yet somehow were able to find their way—
Muttering this was not included in their pay.

Later, sleepless at night, the brain
    spinning
With cracked images, they won't forget
The confusion and the oily dead,
Nor yet the casual knack of living.

ALAN ROSS

181

The Responsibility

I am the man who gives the word,
If it should come, to use the Bomb.

I am the man who spreads the word
From him to them if it should come.

I am the man who gets the word
From him who spreads the word from him.

I am the man who drops the Bomb
If ordered by the one who's heard
From him who merely spreads the word
The first one gives if it should come.

I am the man who loads the Bomb
That he must drop should orders come
From him who gets the word passed on
By one who waits to hear from *him*.

I am the man who makes the Bomb
That he must load for him to drop
If told by one who gets the word
From one who passes it from *him*.

I am the man who fills the till,
Who pays the tax, who foots the bill
That guarantees the Bomb he makes
For him to load for him to drop
If orders come from one who gets
The word passed on to him by one
Who waits to hear it from the man
Who gives the word to use the Bomb.

I am the man behind it all;
I am the one responsible.

PETER APPLETON

Undivided Loyalty

Nothing is worth dying for.
Some people would rather
Be dead than Red.
But I would simply rather
Not be dead.

I would not die for Britain
Or any land. Why should I?
I only happened to be born there.
Emigré, banished, why should I defend
A land I never chose, that never wanted me?

I might have been born anywhere—
In mid-Pacific or in Ecuador.
I would not die for the world.
Jesus was wrong.
Only nothing is worth dying for.

JAMES KIRKUP

★ Performances. Work together in small groups to produce a performance or taped programme on the theme of *War*, linking some of these poems together perhaps with a commentary. Here are a few ideas to start you thinking:

—Several of the poems in this section are written as tiny dramatic scenes. Prepare and rehearse one or more of these using different voices for the different parts. Sassoon's poems *The Rear-Guard* and *The Hero* on pages 170 and 172 are both powerful dramatic evocations of incidents from the horrific trench warfare World War 1. Wilfred Owen's poem *The Dead-Beat* on page 171 tells of another wretched incident from the same time. Both Sassoon and Owen had first hand experience of what they wrote about. Owen was killed by a sniper's bullet in the closing days of the war.

—Hardy's bitter comment in his poem *Christmas: 1924* is a reminder of the horrors of poison gas which was used extensively in trench warfare. It provides a fitting link to a dramatised reading of Owen's description of a mustard gas attack in his poem *Dulce et Decorum Est* on page 175. The latin phrase which is the title of the poem and which ends it is often to be found carved on war memorials. It means 'It is sweet and right to die for one's country'.

—Rupert Brooke's poem *The Soldier* on page 177 may be read by a single voice as a contrasting view to that of Owen or Sassoon.

—*High Wood*, was a bitterly contested strip of ground where eight thousand men fell. Philip Johnstone's poem on page 173 can be read by one person in an unfeeling tour guide's voice.

—Henry Reed's wry poem *Judging Distances* on page 179 is written for two voices: that of the officer giving gunnery practice instruction to his men in brisk no-nonsense military fashion, and the voice of the reluctant soldier who does not want to see the world in military terms. It will take a bit of rehearsal but it is worth persevering.

—In stark contrast to these poems of the First World War you could end your programme with the thought-provoking poem by Peter Appleton, *The Responsibility* which reminds us that such horrors and even worse are not dead but could be unleashed today at the touch of a button. As you can see he builds his poem on the same pattern as the children's nursery rhyme *This is the House that Jack Built* and it needs to be read by several people, each taking one of the parts and all coming together for the final two lines.

★ **Poems and Pictures.** The recruiting posters on pages 172 and 174 were like advertisements for young men to join the army and were to be seen on hoardings everywhere during the First World War. What sort of feelings were they appealing to? Discuss your ideas in pairs and share them with the class. Try to write your own poem beginning with the words of one or other of the posters as your first line. Display your finished poem alongside a copy of the poster or devise your own recruiting poster.

—Goya's painting on pages 184–5 shows one of the many atrocities perpetrated against Spanish citizens by Napoleon's troops in 1808 after the invasion of Spain. Talk in pairs about the details of the picture—the faces of the people, the attitude of the soldiers—and share your ideas. Focus on the scene and try to capture its starkness in a poem of your own.

—Anna Adams was struck by the way the war artist Paul Nash painted crashed planes in the desert as though they were waves on a dead sea (*Todes Meer* in German). There is a copy of another Paul Nash picture on page 177 with the ironic title *We Are Making A New World*. Look carefully at the picture and quickly jot down any images or comparisons it suggests; ask yourself what it is *like*. When you have collected your thoughts on paper try to write a poem of your own which captures your feelings about the picture.

—For many years now we have lived under the shadow of nuclear war and the picture of the detonation of a relatively small nuclear device (see p. 182) can hardly bring home the scale of devastation which would follow a wholesale exchange of weapons. It may help focus your feelings to use the picture as a starting point for a personal piece of writing on the subject.

★ **Research and writing.** Talk to older people you may know —neighbours, relatives, grandparents—who may have memories of the Second World War and try to build up a picture of what it meant to them and their families. You may find it helpful to concentrate on one aspect of the conflict they remember well such as air-raids. What was the first indication of a raid? Did they have shelter? What was it like to be inside waiting and listening? What sounds stick in the memory? Jot down notes from your researches, or, better still, tape-record such memories and use them as either a starting point for a piece of your own writing or as other voices you can fit into your taped programme of war poems.

Cat

cold white cat
waiting
in the lamplight
floodlit
in the dark night
always watching
always waiting
green-eyed and strange
for my return.
the distance
between us
is infinite
you content
in the immediacy
of the cold night
me seeking security
behind a darkened door.
you never purr
or move towards me
to rub against my ankles
but watch and wait
whilst I hurry down the street
fumble for my key
and enter the house.
I shut you out
but you're always there
each morning
each evening
the consciousness
within
my sleep.

SUE KELLY

Cheetah

Indolent and kitten-eyed,
This is the bushveld's innocent—
The stealthy leopard parodied
With grinning, gangling pup-content.

Slouching through the tawny grass
Or loose-limbed lolling in the shade,
Purring for the sun to pass
And build a twilight barricade

Around the vast arena where,
In scattered herds, his grazing prey
Do not suspect in what wild fear
They'll join with him in fatal play;

Till hunger draws slack sinews tight
And vibrant as a hunter's bow:
Then, like a fleck of mottled light,
He slides across the still plateau.

A tremor rakes the herds: they scent
The pungent breeze of his advance;
Heads rear and jerk in vigilant
Compliance with the game of chance

In which, of thousands, only one
Is centred in the cheetah's eye;
They wheel and then stampede, for none
Knows which it is that has to die.

His stealth and swiftness fling a noose
And as his loping strides begin
To blur with speed, he ropes the loose
Buck on the red horizon in.

CHARLES EGLINGTON

Hawk Roosting

I sit in the top of the wood, my eyes closed.
Inaction, no falsifying dream
Between my hooked head and hooked feet:
Or in sleep rehearse perfect kills and eat.

The convenience of the high trees!
The air's buoyancy and the sun's ray
Are of advantage to me;
And the earth's face upward for my inspection.

My feet are locked upon the rough bark.
It took the whole of Creation
To produce my foot, my each feather:
Now I hold Creation in my foot

Or fly up, and revolve it all slowly—
I kill where I please because it is all mine.
There is no sophistry in my body:
My manners are tearing off heads—

The allotment of death.
For the one path of my flight is direct
Through the bones of the living.
No arguments assert my right:

The sun is behind me.
Nothing has changed since I began.
My eye has permitted no change.
I am going to keep things like this.

TED HUGHES

Frogs

Frogs sit more solid
Than anything sits. In mid-leap they are
Parachutists falling
In a free fall. They die on roads
With arms across their chests and
Heads high.

I love frogs that sit
Like Buddha, that fall without
Parachutes, that die
Like Italian tenors.

Above all, I love them because,
Pursued in water, they never
Panic so much that they fail
To make stylish triangles
With their ballet dancer's
Legs.

NORMAN MacCAIG

The Maldive Shark

About the Shark, phlegmatical one,
Pale sot of the Maldive sea,
The sleek little pilot fish, azure and slim
How alert in attendance be.
From his saw-pit of mouth, from his charnel of maw
They have nothing of harm to dread,
But liquidly glide on his ghastly flank
Or before his Gorgonian head;
Or lurk in the port of serrated teeth
In white triple tiers of glittering gates,
And there find a haven when peril's abroad,
An asylum in jaws of the fates!
They are friends; and friendly they guide him to prey,
Yet never partake of the treat—
Eyes and brains to the dotard lethargic and dull,
Pale ravener of horrible meat.

HERMAN MELVILLE

Kangaroo

In the northern hemisphere
Life seems to leap at the air, or skim under the wind
Like stags on rocky ground, or pawing horses, or springy
    scut-tailed rabbits.

Or else rush horizontal to charge at the sky's horizon,
Like bulls or bisons or wild pigs.

Or slip like water slippery towards its ends,
As foxes, stoats, and wolves, and prairie dogs.

Only mice, and moles, and rats, and badgers, and beavers, and
    perhaps bears
Seem belly-plumbed to the earth's mid-navel.
Or frogs that when they leap come flop, and flop to the centre of
    the earth.

But the yellow antipodal Kangaroo, when she sits up,
Who can unseat her, like a liquid drop that is heavy, and just
    touches earth.

The downward drip
The down-urge.
So much denser than cold-blooded frogs.

Delicate mother Kangaroo
Sitting up there rabbit-wise, but huge, plumb-weighted,
And lifting her beautiful slender face, oh! so much more gently
    and finely lined than a rabbit's, or than a hare's,
Lifting her face to nibble at a round white peppermint drop
    which she loves, sensitive mother Kangaroo.

Her sensitive, long, pure-bred face.
Her full antipodal eyes, so dark,
So big and quiet and remote, having watched so many empty
    dawns in silent Australia.

Her little loose hands, and drooping Victorian shoulders.
And then her great weight below the waist, her vast pale belly
With a thin young yellow little paw hanging out, and straggle of
    a long thin ear, like ribbon,
Like a funny trimming to the middle of her belly, thin little
    dangle of an immature paw, and one thin ear.

Her belly, her big haunches
And, in addition, the great muscular python-stretch of her tail.

There, she shan't have any more peppermint drops.
So she wistfully, sensitively sniffs the air, and then turns, goes
    off in slow sad leaps

On the long flat skis of her legs,
Steered and propelled by that steel-strong snake of a tail.

Stops again, half turns, inquisitive to look back.
While something stirs quickly in her belly, and a lean little face
    comes out, as from a window,

Peaked and a bit dismayed,
Only to disappear again quickly away from the sight of the
    world, to snuggle down in the warmth,
Leaving the trail of a different paw hanging out.

Still she watches with eternal, cocked wistfulness!
How full her eyes are, like the full, fathomless, shining eyes of
    an Australian black-boy
Who has been lost so many centuries on the margins of
    existence!

She watches with insatiable wistfulness.
Untold centuries of watching for something to come,
For a new signal from life, in that silent lost land of the South.

Where nothing bites but insects and snakes and the sun, small
    life.
Where no bull roared, no cow ever lowed, no stag cried, no
    leopard screeched, no lion coughed, no dog barked,
But all was silent save for parrots occasionally, in the haunted
    blue bush.

196

Wistfully watching, with wonderful liquid eyes.
And all her weight, all her blood, dripping sack-wise down
    towards the earth's centre,
And the live little-one taking in its paw at the door of her belly.

Leap then, and come down on the line that draws to the earth's
    deep, heavy centre.

D. H. LAWRENCE

Leviathan

A puff-adder, khaki,
fatter than a stocking of pus
except for its short thin tail,
obese and quick
as certain light-footed dancers
took a dozing lizard.

Scaly little monster
with delicate hands and feet
stupidly sluggish in the sun.
Panting, true,
but lizards breathe mostly
as if their lives depended.

Gone.
Enveloped by a slack
wormy yellow bowel.

O Jonah, to tumble to
those sickly deadly depths,
slick walled, implacably black.

DOUGLAS LIVINGSTONE

The Stag

While the rain fell on the November woodland shoulder of
    Exmoor
While the traffic jam along the road honked and shouted
Because the farmers were parking wherever they could
And scrambling to the bank-top to stare through the tree-fringe
Which was leafless,
The stag ran through his private forest.

While the rain drummed on the roofs of the parked cars
And the kids inside cried and daubed their chocolate and fought
And mothers and aunts and grandmothers
Were a tangle of undoing sandwiches and screwed-round
    gossiping heads
Steaming up the windows,
The stag loped through his favourite valley.

While the blue horsemen down in the boggy meadow
Sodden nearly black, on sodden horses,
Spaced as at a military parade,
Moved a few paces to the right and a few to the left and felt
    rather foolish
Looking at the brown impassable river,
The stag came over the last hill of Exmoor.

While everybody high-kneed it to the bank-top all along the road
Where steady men in oilskins were stationed at binoculars,
And the horsemen by the river galloped anxiously this way and
    that
And the cry of hounds came tumbling invisibly with their echoes
    down through the draggle of trees,
Swinging across the wall of dark woodland,
The stag dropped into a strange country.

And turned at the river
Hearing the hound-pack smash the undergrowth, hearing the
    bell-note
Of the voice that carried all the others,
Then while his limbs all cried different directions to his lungs,
    which only wanted to rest,
The blue horsemen on the bank opposite
Pulled aside the camouflage of their terrible planet.

And the stag doubled back weeping and looking for home up a
    valley and down a valley
While the strange trees struck at him and the brambles lashed
    him,
And the strange earth came galloping after him carrying the
    loll-tongued hounds to fling all over him
And his heart became just a club beating his ribs and his own
    hooves shouted with hounds' voices,
And the crowd on the road got back into their cars
Wet-through and disappointed.

TED HUGHES

Elephants

Tonnage of instinctive
Wisdom in tinsel,
Trunks like questions
And legs like tree trunks

On each forehead
A buxom blonde
And round each leg
A jangle of bells,

Deep in each brain
A chart of tropic
Swamp and twilight
Of creepered curtains,

Shamble in shoddy
Finery forward
And make their salaams
To the tiers of people—

Dummies with a reflex
Muscle of laughter
When they see the mountains
Come to Mahomet . . .

Efficacy of engines,
Obstinacy of darkness.   LOUIS MACNEICE

Town Owl

On eves of cold, when slow coal fires,
rooted in basements, burn and branch,
brushing with smoke the city air;

When quartered moons pale in the sky,
and neons glow along the dark
like deadly nightshade on a briar;

Above the muffled traffic then
I hear the owl, and at his note
I shudder in my private chair.

For like an augur he has come
to roost among our crumbling walls,
his blooded talons sheathed in fur.

Some secret lure of time it seems
has called him from his country wastes
to hunt a newer wasteland here.

And where the candelabra swung
bright with the dancers' thousand eyes,
now his black, hooded pupils stare,

And where the silk-shoed lovers ran
with dust of diamonds in their hair,
he opens now his silent wing,

And, like a stroke of doom, drops down,
and swoops across the empty hall,
and plucks a quick mouse off the stair . . .

LAURIE LEE

Lizard

A lizard ran out on a rock and looked up, listening
no doubt to the sounding of the spheres.
And what a dandy fellow! the right toss of a chin for you
and swirl of a tail!

If men were as much men as lizards are lizards
they'd be worth looking at.

D. H. LAWRENCE

Turkeys Observed

One observes them, one expects them;
Blue-breasted in their indifferent mortuary,
Beached bare on the cold marble slabs
In immodest underwear frills of feather.

The red sides of beef retain
Some of the smelly majesty of living:
A half-cow slung from a hook maintains
That blood and flesh are not ignored.

But a turkey cowers in death.
Pull his neck, pluck him, and look—
He is just another poor forked thing,
A skin bag plumped with inky putty.

He once complained extravagantly
In an overture of gobbles;
He lorded it on the claw-flecked mud
With a grey flick of his Confucian eye.

Now, as I pass the bleak Christmas dazzle,
I find him ranged with his cold squadrons:
The fuselage is bare, the proud wings snapped,
The tail-fan stripped down to a shameful rudder.

SEAMUS HEANEY

The Fox

It was twenty years ago I saw the fox
Gliding along the edge of prickling corn,
A nefarious shadow
Between the emerald field and bristling hedge,
On velvet feet he went.

The wind was kind, withheld from him my scent
Till my threaded gaze unmasked him standing there,
The colour of last year's beech-leaves, pointed black,
Poised, uncertain, quivering nose aware
Of danger throbbing through each licking leaf.
One foot uplifted, balanced on the brink
Of perennial fear, the hunter hunted stood.

I heard no alien stir in the friendly wood,
But the fox's sculpted attitude was tense
With scenting, listening, with a seventh sense
Flaring to the alert; I heard no sound
Threaten the morning; and followed his amber stare,
But in that hair-breadth moment, that flick of the eye,
He vanished.

And now, whenever I hear the expectant cry
Of hounds on the empty air,
I look to a gap in the hedge and see him there
Filling the space with fear; the trembling leaves
Are frozen in his stillness till I hear
His leashed-up breathing—how the stretch of time
Contracts within the flash of re-creation!

PHOEBE HESKETH

Heron

A gawky stilt-
ed fossicker* a-
mong reeds, the
gun-grey-green
one, gauntly
watchful cold-
eye, stiff on
single column a
brooding hump
of wind-ruffled
feather-brain
feathering the
blue shall-
ows with one
scaly claw
poised drip-
ping—

      wades
the pebbled lake,
prints the mudflat,
scorns the noi-
sy fancy oy-
stercatchers' talk,
stalks, tall, to
his flat ramshack-
le nest or shack
of slack sticks
with three dull
greeny eggs
by a bul-
rush grove—

till the snaky neck
coils back
and strikes, beak
darts and spears
quick fish,
fish, fish
silvery-rich
fisher-king dish—

and then in the lone-
ly white lazy
hazy afternoon
he rises slowly
in a big zig-
zag heavy over
sultry fens
and windmill vanes,
flapping silently
in the land of wings.

EDWIN MORGAN

*delver

203

The Animals' Carol

Christus natus est! the cock   Christ is born
Carols on the morning dark.

Quando? croaks the raven stiff   When?
Freezing on the broken cliff.

Hoc Nocte, replies the crow   This night
Beating high above the snow.

Ubi? Ubi? booms the ox   Where?
From its cavern in the rocks.

Bethlehem, then bleats the sheep   Bethlehem
Huddled on the winter steep.

Quomodo? the brown hare clicks,   How?
Chattering among the sticks.

Humiliter, the careful wren   Humbly
Thrills upon the cold hedge-stone.

Cur? cur? sounds the coot   Why?
By the iron river-root.

Propter homine, the thrush   For the sake of man
Sings on the sharp holly-bush.

Cui? cui? rings the chough   To whom?
On the strong, sea-haunted bluff.

Mary! Mary! calls the lamb   Mary
From the quiet of the womb.

Praeterea ex quo? cries   Who else?
The woodpecker to pallid skies.

Joseph, breathes the heavy shire   Joseph
Warming in its own blood-fire.

Ultime ex quo? the owl Solemnly begins to call.	Who above all?
De Deo, the little stare Whistles on the hardening air.	Of God
Pridem? pridem? the jack snipe From the stiff grass starts to pipe.	Long ago?
Sic et non, answers the fox Tiptoeing the bitter lough.	Yes and no
Quomodo hoc scire potest? Boldly flutes the robin redbreast.	How do I know this?
Illo in eandem, squeaks The mouse within the barley-sack.	By going there
Quae sarcinae? asks the daw Swaggering from head to claw.	What luggage?
Nulla res, replies the ass, Bearing on its back the Cross.	None
Quantum pecuniae? shrills The wandering gull about the hills.	How much money?
Ne nummum quidem, the rook Caws across the rigid brook.	Not a penny
Nulla resne? barks the dog By the crumbling fire-log.	Nothing at all?
Nil nisi cor amans, the dove Murmurs from its house of love.	Only a loving heart

Gloria in Excelsis! Then
Man is God, and God is Man.

CHARLES CAUSLEY

* **Performances.** *Hawk Roosting* (p. 192) is best read by a single voice. It almost needs to be declaimed from a dominant position in the classroom. How will you speak the series of flat, uncompromising statements? What pace and tone will you adopt? One or two members of the class could try individual performances.

—*The Stag* (p. 198) poses different problems. You'll need to breathe deeply to say the long, run-on lines. Why does Hughes make it so breathless a poem to read? Small groups could prepare a reading, handing on from one reader to the next at the start of each verse as the stag moves through the landscape.

—*Heron* (p. 203) is a long thin poem with many broken words and sharp sounds to suggest the bird's angular movements. Can you capture this sense in the way you read it aloud?

—*The Animals' Carol* (p. 204) needs to be spoken by several voices, either live or taped. Small groups could try out different ways of relating the Latin to the English translation and of characterising the different animals.

* **Poster Poems.** Choose one poem that you like and express what appeals to you about it through designing a poster. Think carefully about the main idea or feeling the poem gives you and try to capture this in your illustration and layout. Include all or part of the text in the design.

Acknowledgments

The editors and publishers would like to thank the following for their kind permission to reproduce copyright material:

Anna Adams: 'Unrecorded Speech' first published in *Encounter* and 'Todes Meer', first published in *Dear Vincent*, both by permission of the author.

Fleur Adcock: 'Leaving the Tate', 'The High Tree', 'Post Office', 'The Telephone Call' and 'For Heidi with Blue Hair' © Fleur Adcock 1986. Reprinted from *The Incident Book* by Fleur Adcock (1986) by permission of Oxford University Press.

John Agard: 'Stereotype', 'Once', 'Listen Mr Oxford don' and 'Limbo Dancer's Soundpoem' by permission of the author.

Peter Appleton: 'The Responsibility' by permission of the author.

Basho: 'Bamboo Grove' from *An Introduction to Haiku* by Harold G. Henderson copyright © 1958 by Harold G. Henderson. Reprinted by permission of Doubleday & Co. Inc.

Rebecca Bazeley: 'Mr Death at the Door', Fitzjohn's School.

John Betjeman: 'Death in Leamington' and 'In Westminster Abbey' from *Collected Poems*, John Murray (Publishers) Ltd.

Billy Bragg: 'The Home Front' © Chappell Music Ltd. Reproduced by permission.

Edwin Brock: 'On Being Chosen for a Schools Anthology' from *With Love from Judith*, Scorpion Press.

Charles Causley: 'Lord Lovelace', 'Ten Types of Hospital Visitor' and 'The Animals' Carol' from *Collected Poems*, David Higham Associates Ltd.

Tony Connor: 'Mrs Root' from *With Love Somehow*, Oxford University Press.

Wendy Cope: 'Triolet' and 'All Purpose Poem for State Occasions' from *Making Cocoa for Kingsley Amis*, reprinted by permission of Faber & Faber Ltd.

e. e. cummings: 'next to of course god america i' from *Complete Poems 1913–1935*, MacGibbon & Kee Ltd.

Keith Douglas: 'Behaviour of Fish in an Egyptian Tea Garden' from *Collected Poems*, reprinted by permission of Faber & Faber Ltd.

Charles Eglington: 'Cheetah' from *The Oxford Book of South African Verse*, Oxford University Press, by permission of the author.

Gavin Ewart: 'British Weather' from *The Young Pobble's Guide to his Toes*, Century Hutchinson Ltd.

Vicki Feaver: 'Days', by permission of the author.

Lawrence Ferlinghetti: 'Christ Climbed Down' and 'Constantly Risking Absurdity' from *A Coney Island of the Mind*, New Directions Publishing Corporation, by permission of the author.

Robert Graves: 'A Civil Servant' from *Collected Poems 1959*, Cassell and Co. Ltd, by permission of the author.

Thomas Hardy: 'Christmas 1924', 'In the Cemetery' and 'Stories of Circumstance in Church' from *Collected Poems*, Macmillan & Co. Ltd and by permission of the estate of Thomas Hardy.

Seamus Heaney: 'Digging', 'Docker', 'Follower', 'Storm on the Island', 'Turkeys Observed' and 'Waterfall' from *Death of a Naturalist*; 'The Forge' from *Door into the Dark*; 'The Railway Children' from *Station Island*, reprinted by permission of Faber & Faber Ltd.

Phoebe Hesketh: 'Prayer for the Sun' from *The Fox*, Rupert Hart-Davis Ltd; 'I Have Not Seen God' from *Between Wheels and Stars*, William Heinemann Ltd, by permission of the author.

Philip Hobsbaum: 'The Place's Fault' from *The Place's Fault and Other Poems*, Macmillan and Co. Ltd.

Miroslav Holub: 'The Lesson' from *Selected Poems*, translated by Ian Milner and George Theiner, Penguin Books Ltd.

Langston Hughes: 'Dream Variation' copyright© 1926 by Alfred A. Knopf Inc. and renewed 1954 by Langston Hughes. Reprinted from *Selected Poems of Langston Hughes*, by permission of Alfred A. Knopf Inc.

Ted Hughes: 'Esther's Tom Cat' and 'November' from *Lupercal*; 'Hawk Roosting' and 'The Thought Fox' from *Hawk in the Rain*; 'Ghost Crabs' from *Wodwo*; 'The Stag' from *Season Songs*, reprinted by permission of Faber & Faber Ltd.

Philip Johnstone: 'High Wood' reprinted from *The Nation* by permission of the *New Statesman*.

Sue Kelly: 'Butterfly' and 'Cat' by permission of the author.

James Kirkup: 'London–Tokyo', 'Rugby League Game' and 'Undivided Loyalty' from *The Prodigal Son*, Oxford University Press, by permission of the author.

Philip Larkin: 'Water' from *The Whitsun Weddings*, reprinted by permission of Faber & Faber Ltd; 'Next Please' and 'Born Yesterday' from *The Less Deceived*, copyright © The Marvell Press; and 'Cut Grass' from *High Windows*, reprinted by permission of Faber & Faber Ltd.

D. H. Lawrence: 'Baby Tortoise', 'Kangaroo', 'Lizard' and 'When I Went to the Film' from *The Complete Poems of D. H. Lawrence*, William Heinemann Ltd, by permission of Laurence Pollinger Ltd and the estate of the late Mrs Frieda Lawrence.

Laurie Lee: 'Sunken Evening' and 'Town Owl' from *My Many Coated Man*, André Deutsch.

John Lennon: 'Imagine'. Words by John Lennon © 1971 Lenono Music, Chappell Music Ltd, London. Words reproduced by permission.

Denise Levertov: 'The Secret' from *O Taste and See*, Laurence Pollinger Ltd.

Alun Lewis: 'All Day it Has Rained' from *Raiders Dawn*, George Allen and Unwin Ltd.

Douglas Livingstone: 'Leviathan' from *Sjambok and Other Poems*, Oxford University Press.

Liz Lochhead: 'Laundrette' from *Dreaming Frankenstein and Poems*, Polygon.

Norman MacCaig: 'Frogs' from *Surroundings*, The Hogarth Press Ltd.

Roger McGough: 'First Haiku of Spring' from *Melting into the Foreground* published by Penguin, reprinted by permission of A. D. Peters & Co. Ltd.

Louis MacNeice: 'Elephants' from *Collected Poems*, reprinted by permission of Faber & Faber Ltd.

Edwin Morgan: 'Heron', by permission of the author; 'Glasgow Sonnet' from *Selected Poems* by permission of Carcanet Press Ltd.

Grace Nichols: 'Hey There, Now!', 'The Fat Black Woman Goes Shopping' and 'Be a Butterfly' from *The Fat Black Woman's Poems*, Virago Ltd.

Norman Nicholson: 'Rising Five' from *The Pot Geranium*, reprinted by permission of Faber & Faber Ltd.

Wilfred Owen: 'The Dead-Beat', 'Dulce et Decorum Est' and 'From My Diary, July 1914' from *The Collected Poems of Wilfred Owen*, Chatto & Windus Ltd, by permission of Mr Harold Owen.

Brian Patten: 'The Projectionist's Nightmare' from *Little Johnny's Confession*, George Allen & Unwin; 'Frogs in the Wood' from *New Volume*, by permission of the author.

Tom Paxton: 'What did you Learn in School Today?' © 1966 Harmony Music Ltd, 19/20 Poland Street, London W1V 3DD. International Copyright secured. All rights reserved. Used by permission.

Sylvia Plath: 'Balloons' from *Ariel*, Faber & Faber Ltd, by permission of Olwyn Hughes.
Peter Porter: 'A Consumer's Report' from *The Last of England*, Oxford University Press.
Ezra Pound: 'Meditatio' from *Collected Shorter Poems*, reprinted by permission of Faber & Faber Ltd.
Craig Raine: 'The Window Cleaner' © Craig Raine, 1978. Reprinted from *The Onion, Memory* by Craig Raine (1978) by permission of Oxford University Press.
Henry Reed: 'Judging Distances' from *A Map of Verona*, Jonathan Cape Ltd, by permission of the author.
Theodore Roethke: 'Orchids' from *Collected Poems*, reprinted by permission of Faber & Faber Ltd.
John La Rose: 'Not From Here' from *Breaklight*, Hamish Hamilton Ltd.
Alan Ross: 'Embankment Before Snow' from *To Whom It May Concern (Poems 1952–57)*, Hamish Hamilton Ltd, © 1958 Alan Ross; 'Survivors' from *Something of the Sea*, Derek Verschoyle.
Colin Rowbotham: 'Vase/Faces', 'Alphabeast' and 'December', by permission of the author.
Siegfried Sassoon: 'The Hero' and 'The Rear-Guard' from *Collected Poems*, Faber & Faber Ltd, by permission of Mr George Sassoon.
Vernon Scannell: 'After the Fireworks' from *Walking Wounded*, Eyre and Spottiswoode Ltd, by permission of the author.
Stephen Spender: 'Word' from *Collected Poems*, reprinted by permission of Faber & Faber Ltd.
R. S. Thomas: 'The Maker' and 'Poetry for Supper' from *Poetry for Supper*, Rupert Hart-Davis Ltd.
John Updike: 'Bendix' from *Telephone Poles and Other Poems*, André Deutsch.
Glyne Walrond: 'Blackness' from *The Children's Voice*, Stockwell.
Humbert Wolfe: 'The Grey Squirrel' by permission of Ann Wolfe.

Every effort has been made to trace the copyright holders of the following poems:

Jennifer Armitage: 'To Our Daughter'
Richard Armour: 'To a Human Skeleton'
Basil Bunting: 'What the Chairman Told Tom'
Vladimir Mayakovsky: 'Talking with the Taxman about Poetry'
Adrian Mitchell: 'I Like that Stuff' and 'Back in the Playground Blues'
G. Okara: 'Once Upon a Time'
Raymond Souster: 'Flight of the Roller Coaster'

Thanks are also due to Mr John Teasey, Head of English, Robert Mays' School, Odiham, Hampshire for the pupils' readings of Brian Patten's 'Frogs in the wood'.

The editors and publishers would also like to thank the following for permission to reproduce illustrations:

Natural History Photographic Agency (pp. 12 and 200); © ADAGP, Paris and DACS, London 1988: 'The Healer' (1937) by René Magritte (p. 19); Museum der Bildenden Künste, Leipzig: 'Die Lebensstufen' by Caspar David Friedrick (pp. 20–1); Mantis Wildlife Films, Australia (p. 24); The Museum of Modern Art, New York: 'Landscape: the persistence of memory' by Salvador Dali (pp. 26–7); The Science Photo Library (p. 31); The Commonwealth Institute (p. 39); Mr Harold Owen, Chatto and Windus Ltd and the British Museum: First draft and fourth and final draft of 'Anthem for Dead Youth' by Wilfred Owen (pp. 50–1); © 1988 M. C. Escher Heirs/Cordon Art, Baarn, Holland: 'Cirkellimiet IV' by M. C. Escher (p. 66); © ADAGP 1987: 'Bather Between Light and Darkness' (1935) by René Magritte (p. 69); the Huntington Library, San Marino, California (pp. 100–1); Mme Sonia Delaunay and Sotheby & Co.: 'The Runner' by R. Delaunay (p. 111); Phaidon Press Ltd (p. 119); Glen Baxter: illustration from *Glen Baxter His Life: The Years of Struggle* copyright © 1983 by Glen Baxter, published by Thames & Hudson (p. 126); The Ashmolean Museum, Oxford (pp. 128–9); Birmingham City Museum and Art Gallery and the Royal Academy of Arts: 'February Fill-Dyke' by B. W. Leader RA (pp. 132–3); Eric Crichton Photos (p. 135); Topham Picture Library (p. 136); Barnaby's Picture Library (p. 140); Bill Brandt: 'Wet Roofs' (p. 143); The John Hillelson Agency: 'Battered Mannequin' (p. 162); Imperial War Museum: First World War recruiting posters (pp. 172, 174); and 'We are making a new world' by Paul Nash (p. 177); UK Atomic Energy Authority: 'One of Britain's atomic explosions' (p. 182); The Prado Museum, Madrid: 'Shooting of May 3rd' by Goya, 1808 (pp. 184–5); Neville Cooper: 'Old Lady with a Cat' (p. 188); ARDEA London Limited (p. 195); The Tate Gallery: 'Todes Meer' by Paul Nash (p. 178).